Ca$h from Square Foot Gardening

by Mel Bartholomew

STOREY

Storey Communications, Inc.
Schoolhouse Road
Pownal, Vermont 05261

Designed by Cindy McFarland
Cover photo by Didier Delmas
Photographs by Didier Delmas and Roger Griffith
Illustrations by Tara Deveraux and Cindy McFarland

Printed in the United States by Alpine Press
Third Printing, November, 1985

Library of Congress Catologing-in-Publication Data

Bartholomew, Mel.
  Cash from square foot gardening.

  1. Vegetable Gardening. 2. Square foot gardening.
3. Vegetable gardening--Economic aspects. 4. Square foot
gardening--Economic aspects. I. Title.
SB321.B277 1985   635'.068   85-50122

ISBN 0-88266-396-8
ISBN 0-88266-395-X (pbk.)

Acknowledgments

Turning an idea into reality takes the help of many people. In particular, I'd like to thank my good friend Bill Kulkman, who devoted a considerable amount of time during the early days of developing this idea. To Wayne Clifton, a special thanks for testing the idea in a different part of the country, and to Hank Elias for building and maintaining the garden we used on our T.V. show.

Barbara Panoras deserves a great deal of credit for pulling the manuscript together in the early editing stages. But most of all, I'd like to thank all those chefs I've spoken to who enthusiastically said, "I'll buy all the fresh produce you can bring me."

They really made this idea come to life and are out there waiting for you to come see them.

Contents

Chapter 1

Do You Really Want a Part-time Business?

$ Anyone who picks up this book is going to say, "Sure, I'd love to have a part-time business. Why, I can picture it now—my very own piece of the American dream. I'd be my own boss, with no one to answer to, no one to take orders from, no one to tell me what to do or how to do it. And, to top it off, I'd have a separate source of income. This could mean financial security and, with a lot of hard work and a little luck, financial independence.

"Think of all the things I could buy with that money, of all the places I could afford to visit."

If you'll come down to earth for just a minute, I'll repeat the question: Do you *really* want a part-time business? I mean, *really*. Are you willing to spend the time and effort necessary to make it work? Can you discipline yourself so things will get done without a boss checking up on you? Do you have the "stick-to-itiveness" to give your part-time business attention long after the first flush of excitement fades? It's like adopting a new pet: someone will have to feed and bathe it, train it, take care of it when it's sick, let it in and out of the house—all the things we don't think about when we're cuddling it on the way home from the pet shop.

If you're willing to put in the time and want to earn extra cash, then I'll show you how to start the perfect home business. I'll explain in detail how you can earn several thousand dollars a year working in your spare time (just a couple of hours a day) right in your own backyard.

And, what's more, you'll get paid for doing something you love to do: garden. It doesn't matter whether you're a beginner or an expert, young or old, whether you live in the city or the suburbs, own your own home or rent an apartment, live in the North, South, East, or West, this program works everywhere and for just about everyone.

You Decide the Terms

I'm going to show you how to start a part-time business on *your own terms*. In other words, you will be the boss. You will decide how many hours you want to work. You will choose the days of the week and the times of the day. You will decide how hard you want to work. Just think, instead of accepting a part-time job on Tuesday, Thursday, and Saturday nights from six to eleven, when they want you and having to do whatever they want you to do, now you can be the boss and make the decisions. In effect, you can write your own ticket to freedom and happiness.

And if, after starting, you aren't making enough money and want to expand, there's no problem. You can spend as much spare time as you desire with direct, profitable results. On the other hand, if you find yourself spending more hours than you really want to, it's just as easy to cut back to a more comfortable level.

If you find it hard to imagine getting paid for something you do for enjoyment, imagine harder. Believe me, you will soon get used to the idea of earning money for something you love doing. Soon, with a little effort and direction, you will be turning your spare time into cash—big cash.

Why Square Foot Gardening
Is the Ideal Business

Close to home	Flexible hours
Little cash required	No expensive equipment
Enjoyable	Easy to manage
Run business yourself	Few supplies needed
Product is high in demand	Profitable
Little waste	Uncomplicated

"But I have no spare time," you say. Nonsense. Everyone has spare time. Pick up any magazine—especially one for working women—and I guarantee you'll find an article on how to use your spare time. Some will advise you to set aside the first and last hour of your day to pursue a special interest; some recommend taking three or four fifteen-minute breaks during the day for exercise or relaxation. All this can be done without interfering with your daily schedule or your productivity. In fact, it's supposed to increase your production by giving you a new lease on life. Well, your part-time business can be handled that same way, and if you take those other few hours a day everyone has available—you know, a little before or after work, after dinner, or even later in the evening—that's all you need.

In fact, with a cash garden, you don't have to set aside time every day. Some people set aside two or three days during the week, while others use their weekends. Remember, you're the boss now. It's up to you to decide how you want to divide your time.

Tax Advantages

Your part-time business will also bring you another reward at the end of each year (more accurately, around April 15) in the form of several big income tax deductions. The federal tax laws not only allow, but actually encourage you to deduct from your income all the expenses of running your business. A portion of car depreciation, repairs, insurance, and gas; garden tools and supplies such as peat moss, pails, pots, planting six-packs, vermiculite, and fencing; special clothing such as gloves and boots; harvesting equipment and containers; electricity, water...why, even the seeds and plants you buy can be deducted. In addition you'll even be able to deduct office equipment such as a calculator and a typewriter.

You'll even be able to write off a portion of your house and garage expenses. That means really big bucks for heat, electricity, and water. It's all very legal and legitimate, too. The government wants you to be successful in your part-time business. After all, that's what America is all about, isn't it? Everyone deserves an opportunity to be successful and happy. Besides, if your business is successful, it will ultimately generate more tax revenue and increase the gross national product.

Even if this were to be classified as just a hobby business, you can deduct all of your direct and indirect expenses for three years without making a profit. Then you must make a profit the next two years. The years don't have to occur in that sequence. If you claim deductions on your return, you have to earn a profit in two out of every five years.

But you're going to do better than that, I just know it. I am going to show you how to have a profit every year.

Your Qualifications

Are you qualified to run a part-time business?

First of all, don't get scared and jump to the conclusion that you aren't qualified. Read on and let's see whether any fears you might have can't be easily resolved.

THREE REASONS MOST NEW BUSINESSES FAIL

Reasons for Failing	How About Cash Gardening?
1. Money: Starting costs too high; not enough money coming in.	Starting costs as low as $50.
2. Lack of experience or ability.	Square foot gardening is so easy a beginner becomes an expert in no time at all.
3. Lack of business the first year.	This method assures a continuous profit before you start; your customer will buy everything that you can raise.

Most people say at first, "But I've never run a business. I wouldn't know the first thing about how to go about getting started, how to set it up, or even how to keep it going."

Not true. All of us already run businesses—our own personal businesses, our personal lives. You buy things every day, paying in cash or by check, you charge things and pay when you get the bill, you sit down once a month to look over all those bills and decide which ones to pay now and which ones to hold off on, you mail-order clothing or gifts, you plan meals in advance, you even make big decisions about vacations, make the reservations and then carry them out. And whether you're on a vacation or a quick jaunt to the local shopping mall, you're continually making decisions on where to go, whom to buy from, who can give you the best service or products for your money. Every time you eat out, you decide on where to go, what to order, whether the bill is correct, how much to tip. Don't tell me you can't handle a small part-time business. You're doing it right now.

What's Involved

Now that you're no longer worried about being qualified, let's go on to the next question: what's really involved in a part-time business? The answer is there are a lot of things, just as in daily living. If you look at each one separately, one at a time, they're just a lot of simple steps. When you put them all together, they become the daily functioning of a business. Even initial establishment is nothing more than a step-by-step process of recognizing, evaluating, deciding, and then acting. I'm going to take you through each step of the cash gardening business. By the time you finish this book, you'll know all there is to know about it. You'll just have to make slight adjustments for your area, your situation, and your desires.

Ask yourself these questions:

"Do I really want to earn extra cash?"

"Do I enjoy gardening?"

If your answers are "yes," the rest is easy. You have to be serious and willing to apply your full talent, interest, and enthusiasm. Of course, there are bound to be some slow or discouraging times when you feel like giving up, and for these you'll need that "stick-to-itiveness," some determination to get over the rough spots.

Any business requires time, too, and you must be willing to give it that time, especially at first. There will be times when everyone else is off playing and you have to tend to business. At these times, try to remember it's not really business, it's just your old hobby, gardening. You will want to keep adequate records, invest the necessary time on a fairly regular schedule, and be determined to do a good job.

Good Boss Needed

Whether you can be a good boss, much less your own boss, is a question you'll soon be able to answer. As the boss (that's you), you'll want to insist your employee (you again) is on time, productive, knowledgeable, honest, diligent, friendly, and trustworthy. If your employee isn't, it's your job as boss to point them out and to help train that person to do better. Of course, the first step is to recognize that there's something lacking before you can point it out or help correct it, and sometimes that's very hard when you're dealing with yourself. We don't often recognize our own flaws. They just don't seem to show up in a mirror. You have to be constantly on the alert. One rule of thumb is to ask yourself, "If I hired someone and this is what he did, would I be satisfied?"

WHEN TO START

A good thing about the cash garden business is that you can start at any season of the year.

If it's winter, you should plan, organize, buy supplies, and sign up your buyers.

If it's spring, you should do all of the winter steps and start planting.

If it's summer, you should gradually convert your garden to a cash garden, and plan on going bigger next year.

Fall is the best time to get your soil and new garden layout ready. It's also the best time to sign up buyers.

Now is the time to decide how much time and energy you want to devote to this new business, and how much space you have available.

Is It Worthwhile?

Are you asking yourself, "Will it all be worthwhile?" The answer, without question is going to be "yes." Just think of the pride and self-satisfaction you'll have in becoming your own boss—something everyone desires but few actually accomplish. The rewards in self-esteem alone just can't be measured. It's a chance that doesn't come along often; for some people, not once in a lifetime. And the best part is that you don't have to quit your job. No big financial risks, no moving to another state, none of the headaches normally associated with a career or job change. Yes, it will all be worthwhile—if you want to gain control over your financial life by producing some extra income, if you're willing to be your own boss, be independent, and shape your own future. And you'll also be helping others by providing freshly grown, succulent vegetables—a direct link to a better and healthier way of life.

People will even live longer because of you. That's really a worthwhile accomplishment. Regardless of your present situation or circumstances, if you want to have your own business, you will succeed. In fact, you can't miss.

Making Decisions

In starting any home business, certain factors must be considered. The most basic is choosing a type of business you think you'll enjoy, as well as one you're going to be good at.

Next, you must consider how much free time you have, whether there is a market for your product, how much competition you will have, and what you need to get started. Will you have to rent a store front to sell your product or will an ad in the paper suffice? Can you work at home or will you have to travel? How much money will be needed to get started, and will you lose it all if the business isn't successful? Will you need help, special services, permits, supplies? Is it a year-round or a seasonal business, and how does that tie in with your schedules and preferences? You wouldn't want to start a wreath business if you like your December holidays free for family activities, or a pool-cleaning business if you like to travel during the summer.

The perfect business would be one that is inexpensive to start, has few government regulations or involvements, is easy to run, and brings top dollar for your product (which, in turn, should have little or no waste or leftovers, and be easy to sell). The most convenient location is at or near your home. This new business should not require lots of special or expensive equipment, staff, or personnel, but should be something you can operate out of your own home. If it is suitable for a majority of the population and will work just as well in any location or state, all the better.

The Perfect Business

I can't think of any home business better qualified than the cash garden idea. Let me tell you why. First, you can start right in your own backyard. Even the smallest of yards will do. Next, it requires little equipment and materials. You probably already have most of them, or can borrow or rent them very cheaply. You can even get such items as harvest baskets and equipment for free if you know where to ask (see chapter fifteen). You'll have the ideal product to sell, as fresh produce is in big demand and will command top dollar. I'll even explain how you can charge full retail price while others are getting wholesale or half price, and I'll show you how to avoid waste.

Backyards like this one offer ample space for cash gardening.

The cash garden is a business almost anyone who loves to garden can run. No special skills or talents are required, and since you're working at home, you don't need to buy extra clothes, travel, hire a babysitter, or worry about your pets. You can hear the phone ring (if you want to) or catch the mailman when he comes. You'll even be home when that plumber finally arrives, but now you can get something done while you wait for him.

Little Red Tape

Persons who start businesses dread looking into the federal, state, county, and local government regulations. You'll be pleasantly surprised to learn that there will be little, if any, red tape, rules, regulations, or government interference connected with a cash garden. You'd think that because you're raising food, that all the authorities would try to get into the act. But unless you've got a really big business, or are shipping across state lines, or are involved in the processing, freezing, or product-making aspects of food, no one will probably bother you.

Just to make sure, call your local county agricultural agent or the county Extension Service. Be right up front with them. Tell them exactly what you plan to do, and ask if there are any regulations you should know about, or permits that might be required. While you're talking, ask for a list of varieties of vegetables that do well in your area. The county agents are there to help you grow vegetables successfully. They spend most of their time with farmers, but should be happy to give you all the advice they can. Take down the name of the person you speak with and ask if you can get back to him if you have any questions.

This was a lawn until we established eight 4 X 12-foot beds.

Your Customers

You may have the greatest idea going, but it won't succeed unless someone buys your product. The bottom line is this: do you have a market for your fresh produce? Your next step must be to think about customers and markets.

There are many ways to sell your produce, from selling to your neighbors who stop by (they could phone in an order ahead of time, but then they don't get to squeeze the tomatoes) to setting up a table at the weekly farmers' market. However, I'm not going to recommend either of these ideas. Your market is so important; it can easily mean the difference between success and failure. I've devoted a chapter to this subject, and when you read it, several ideas will probably appeal to you. My advice is to consider the choices very carefully and to select a market only after a great deal of study. You want to be successful, and your market will be the single most important factor in reaching that goal.

Backup Needed

Consider your support system before you start your business. What happens when you can't be there because of work, vacation, illness, or some other emergency? Can you count on a neighbor, friend, or family member to help out? There will always be a few people looking over your fence, at first wondering what you're up to, and later telling you how you could do it better. Why not press them into action when the need arises? Ask them if they'd come over to water or cover the plants should you need help, and show them how to do it so they'll be prepared. You may never need their services, but better safe than sorry.

Talk It Over

I would suggest that you talk over your ideas with a spouse or gardening or business friend and see what he or she thinks. You'll probably hear a lot of reasons why you shouldn't start such a business, or why it won't work. Don't let that discourage you. Think through the ideas and objections, determine whether they have any validity—then go ahead and start your business. If you're truly determined to work hard and if you follow my advice carefully, you can't miss. Your business will be a success.

Chapter 2
Cash from the Square Foot Garden

$\boxed{\$}$ Let's assume that you're beginning to like the idea of starting a part-time business at home, with the goal of earning a few extra thousand dollars a year. Now that you're familiar with the requirements of the perfect part-time business, you may even agree that a backyard cash garden fulfills many or all of these requirements. But why, you ask, should it be a square foot garden? Some of you may even be wondering what a square foot garden is. For those of you who have never read my first book, *Square Foot Gardening,* or seen the nationally televised PBS series of the same name, here's a brief summary of how it all started.

The Beginning

The idea of a new method of gardening came to me when I retired from my own consulting engineering business several years ago and became involved with a local gardening club. Since I had more free time than most members, everyone always looked at me when the club needed a volunteer. Soon I found myself organizing and running a new community garden. Then I began to teach gardening techniques to its members.

I must admit that at first I taught single row gardening because that was all I'd ever known. But as I watched everyone garden, I began to question that old-fashioned method. I found it to be illogical and inefficient in terms of time, space, cost, production—you name it. After asking all of the experts around the country why we still use the single row method, the only answer I got was,

"Because that's the way we've always done it." That alone was enough to make me say, "There's got to be a better way."

BASICS OF SQUARE FOOT GARDENING

1. Create permanent four-foot square garden blocks, with narrow aisles all around.

2. Put a border—lumber is fine—around each one.

3. Loosen existing soil and fill with the best soil mix possible.

4. Add metal frames to north side of blocks to support vertical vegetables—cucumbers, tomatoes, squash, and melons.

5. Plan and plant your garden in single square-foot units.

6. Harvest when crops are at their peak.

7. Enrich soil and plant new crops immediately.

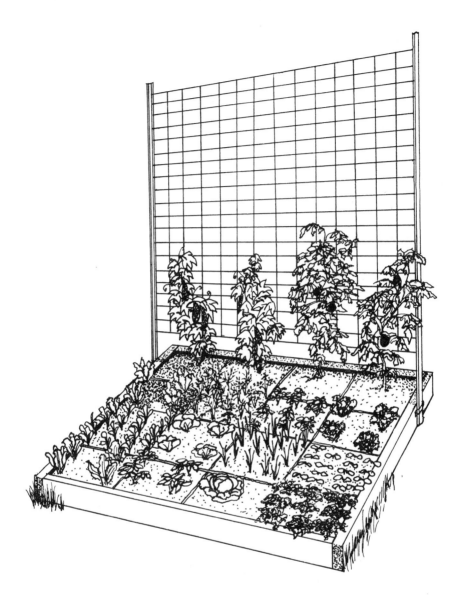

A typical square foot garden offers a variety of vegetables.

The New Method

After a few years of experimentation, I came up with the square foot method, a system so simple a beginner can catch on in just a few hours. It takes only 20 percent of the growing space of a conventional garden. Drudgery is out, for by eliminating 80 percent of the space you automatically eliminate 80 percent of the watering, weeding, fertilizing, and all the other chores that get people very discouraged by mid-summer. Taking care of that remaining 20 percent becomes so easy that it's hard to convince old-timers that it works. In fact, I don't even try to convince them anymore.

It's the beginner, the person who has always wanted to garden, the person who tried but gave up because the work became drudgery—it's *those* approximately 45 million Americans I want to reach, to show them how easy and fun square foot gardening is. Through the weekly national PBS-TV show, this has happened. Oh, I still get an occasional letter from someone, one of those old-timers (I don't necessarily mean old in years, just by habit and attitude) saying it just won't work, it's too easy. So I say they're probably right (but don't tell the millions of Americans who are already enjoying their square foot gardens).

While I was experimenting and developing the square foot system, I ran into a lot of people who were having trouble making ends meet. This was in 1975, in the days of a national recession. We had high unemployment and extreme inflation, and the price of gas shot up from thirty cents to over $1.30 per gallon. I kept thinking that one answer would be for everyone across the country to start a home food garden as they did during World War II. But many people came up to me and said, "You know, I was a kid in the forties. My parents made me work in our Victory Garden, and I've hated gardening ever since."

Even though our Victory Gardens may have helped us win the war, they also helped give gardening a bad name. Memories of hoeing long single rows of corn and beans, getting hot and dusty, lugging pails of water, picking and shelling peas until we could scream... it was just too much.

Why Grow So Much?

Which brought me to my next question: why did we grow so much and why was it all ready to harvest at the same time? There must be a better way to garden. We're still being taught by most experts to grow crops in long, single rows, and now the latest fad is double or triple rows or even wide rows, as if a single row fifteen feet long didn't produce enough lettuce all at once. What's a home gardener going to do with thirty heads of leaf lettuce in one week? Now we're supposed to grow triple rows and raise ninety heads. Come on, America, let's wake up and throw all that lettuce back at the experts.

Single row gardening is merely a hand-me-down of commercial farming. All those single rows with a three-foot path between them, on both sides, no less, were planned so the tractor could get in.

But most Americans don't own tractors and don't even want to, so why waste so much space? If leaf lettuce can be planted six inches apart in a row, why does the next row have to be two or three feet away? It doesn't, of course.

A lot of space is wasted when vegetables are planted in single rows.

How It Works

Square foot gardening offers you a controlled method of planting and wastes no space. Your garden has several four-foot squares of planting space, each with an aisle all the way around it. You reach into your planting area, you don't step on it. By walking only in the aisles, you keep your growing soil loose and friable, instead of being packed down.

Then you work your garden one square foot at a time. If one square foot of radishes (sixteen) isn't enough, you plant two square feet and get thirty-two radishes. It's that simple. If one square foot of ruby lettuce (four heads) isn't enough for one week, plant two square feet and get eight heads. Cabbage is larger than lettuce and each head requires a square foot, so plant the same number of square feet as you want cabbage.

If a cutworm gets one or two of those plants, have a few extra transplants standing by, or plant a few extras, just in case. But not a whole thirty-foot row of them. If you feel you can accept the loss of one or two plants, then immediately replant that square foot with another crop. Either way, your garden will remain full and continually productive with every square foot being planted, grown, harvested, and then replanted with a second and even a third crop. Depending on your choice of crops and your area of the country, you might get four or five crops per year from every square foot.

Controlled Harvest

Controlled planting means a controlled harvest: four heads of lettuce a week, nine bunches of spinach, sixteen radishes, one head of cabbage.

This is more in keeping with today's way of shopping and eating. It just doesn't make sense to grow more than you need, then to hurriedly try to can, freeze, or worst of all, eat all those extra vegetables.

That's the basic idea of the system. There are some adaptions we'll discuss later for growing a cash garden.

Grown Locally

As I was developing, testing, and perfecting my square foot system, the economy kept going downhill, and folks were having it harder than ever. I began to wonder. Why not have a small, local home business selling vegetables? Why should farmers grow crops in one state and ship them in refrigerated cars clear across the country when the same produce could be grown locally and delivered fresh just a few miles to its destination? It seemed logical that combining square foot gardening with the concept of selling vegetables locally could provide a solution to the economic crunch we're all hearing about.

Need a Market

But how to sell, and to whom? That was the next question. As a businessman, I knew you had to have a good market or you didn't have a business. It doesn't matter whether you knit sweaters or grow spinach, if there isn't someone, or better yet a lot of people, who want what you're producing and are willing to pay for it, you have a hobby, not a business.

So I sat down and approached the problem from the purely business standpoint. Since the first step usually is to see what others have done, I checked all the books I could find on selling garden produce. What a collection. They all promised dramatic results, including cash, but I soon found out that they weren't very practical. One was a collection of a company's magazine articles over the past ten years, put together as the chapters of a book. Boy, was that outdated. Another went into great detail on how to design and pave a parking lot for a roadside stand. Can you imagine how few people would find that information useful? The rest of the stories told how someone took a bushel basket of huge zucchinis into a restaurant and asked, "How much will you give me for this?" The answer was usually $2.50.

So again, I knew I had to find a better way, one that just about anyone could use. I first named it backyard farming, and I set out to prove it would work. After raising the vegetables in a square foot garden, I tested every market I could think of, with the sole exception of driving down the street in my vintage truck, ringing a bell. After making a few adjustments and a few more trials, I came up with the requirements for a foolproof system and named it Cash from Square Foot Gardening.

The Final Test

To make sure it wasn't just a fluke, or the results of my own ambition and drive, I rented a vacant lot and hired three people to grow and sell the vegetables. They were a newlywed young woman, a middle-aged housewife, and a retired gentleman who had been a concert pianist. They worked with great enthusiasm and quickly learned the system. None was an expert gardener. In fact, two were fairly new to gardening, but they all loved what they were doing, and it worked. The results: more than $1 per square foot profit. And remember, this was several years ago. It worked so well that I knew I would have to write a book about it, to share this experience with all who love gardening and want to earn some extra money from their backyards.

This book would have been written four years ago, except for one thing—television. No, not because I spent too much time watching football games or soap operas, but because I ended up on PBS television with my own weekly program. Some say that the book should have been called, "How to Get on TV When You're Just a Retired Gardener Puttering in Your Yard." It's been extremely exciting, but very time-consuming. When the TV show was on around the country year-round and everything was going smoothly, I knew the time had come to write this book.

Works Again

But before I began writing I tested again to make sure the idea was still good. This time it was in another part of the country and with different people. It worked even better and with dramatically increased results. The profits were up to $4 and $5 per square foot.

I'm so convinced that this method works in any part of the country that I want you to try it. You don't have to make it a big deal or a large operation. Some people start with only one crop, such as radishes or lettuce, while others start small with a selected variety of salad crops. The main thing is if you wanted to do something like this, now is the time. If you list all of the conditions of your present situation, and then review what you consider is a perfect part-time business, I think you'll agree that this could be it, whether you're looking for extra money, companionship, involvement, success, or simply something to fill your leisure time.

This system will work for you while all others are impractical for most people. Why? This is the first system designed by a businessman rather than a farmer or gardener. All the others tell how to raise crops, then, almost as an afterthought, tell how to sell them, suggesting a roadside stand or a farmers' market, methods that just aren't practical for most gardeners.

This system is aimed at a common, readily available, yet virtually untapped market. That makes it a sound business. The second point is that by following the square foot system, you eliminate 80 percent of the drudgery, work, expense, and space of conventional gardening, yet reap the same amount. That makes it practical for just about anyone, young or old, busy or with time to spare.

To those of you who ask, "Why square foot gardening?" the answer is, "Because it is the most foolproof way of growing the largest and most uniform harvest in the least amount of space with the least amount of work." If you do not have a square foot garden, read the next chapter in detail as well as the original Square Foot Garden book. If you are already growing a square foot garden, the next chapter will bring you up to date with the innovations and improvements as well as the special adaptations for cash growing.

For easier planting, strings mark the square feet in this garden.

Chapter 3

The Basics of Square Foot Gardening

Even though square foot gardening took only two years to develop, it has tremendous advantages over the old-fashioned single row method which is hundreds of years old. That's because this new system is designed for a new society, a new way of life.

Today, our leisure time is spent away from home, at some place you must drive to. With this dramatic shift in the use of leisure time and the trend toward more working couples, the average American doesn't have the time to tend a large garden, yet we're still being taught to garden by the same old-fashioned, single row method, with an occasional new idea, such as "Plant two rows together to save space."

Most of us don't live out in the country with acres and acres, we don't have tractors in our gardens, nor do we care to devote our time and energy to a large garden. In addition, we don't can and preserve food as we used to. We don't even shop as we did thirty years ago. Today's method of growing the square foot way is as different from single row gardening as today's shopping malls and supermarkets are from old-time corner butcher shops and the local grocery.

When I thought about all this, and realized that we're on the threshold of the electronic age, yet still gardening with an antiquated, inefficient system, I knew I had to find a better way. After a few years of trial and experimentation, the square foot gardening system was born. I think you're going to like it.

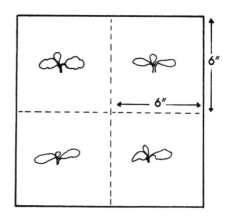

A square foot divided in half each way makes four spaces for leaf lettuce, Swiss chard, and kale.

Needs of Plants

I started by analyzing what a plant needs to produce a perfect crop. First, a good, loose, rich soil that drains well yet holds moisture and nutrients for the roots when they need them. Second, adequate growing space. Third, no competition from seedlings, weeds, pests, or tree roots. Fourth, lots of sun and moisture.

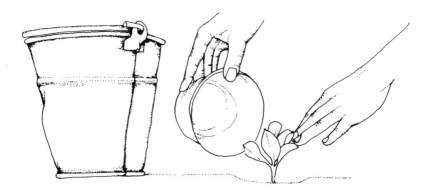

The shallow depression around this plant makes watering more effective.

Needs of Gardener

Next I looked at the needs of the home gardener. Again, not many. First, a small but continuous harvest. Second, a garden that is easy to care for, yet attractive. Those two things would satisfy almost everyone. Square foot gardening meets all four of the plants' requirements and provides the home gardener with the two things that he's looking for. Let's see how.

If you're like most gardeners, you start out every spring full of enthusiasm and good intentions. But we all plant too large a garden, too many seeds, too many plants, and too many rows. Then, as the season progresses, the weeds and bugs take over, resulting in an unsightly mess.

This in turn robs our plants of most of the water and nutrients available, causing a further reduction in productivity. We then tramp all over the garden soil, packing it down. We are left with nothing but a messy, weedy patch and a small harvest. What harvest there is comes in spurts—all the lettuce at one time, for example. It's feast or famine.

A startling fact is that most gardeners end up harvesting very little of what they planted. As the summer wears on, they become dissatisfied and disinterested in their gardens, despite all their hard work. This happens every year to well over half of the people who start a garden.

Plant Requirements	Single Row	Square Foot
Rich, loose, friable soil	Only after working six years	Perfect the first year
Sufficient growing space	Usually too much	Just right
No weeds, pests, or tree roots	Too much of everything	No competition
Adequate sun and moisture	Hard to adjust	Easily provided

Home Gardener Desires		
Manageable but continuous harvest	Feast or famine	Easily controlled
Carefree and attractive garden	Mostly weeds	Needs only one hour per week

A Better Way

That's when I decided there had to be a better way, one more suited to our way of life, a method that produced an attractive garden without a lot of work, one that was so simple and easy to understand that anyone could garden regardless of experience.

First, we would lay the garden out in a pattern of several planting squares, each four feet by four feet. They could be flat or raised. Aisles twelve to twenty-four inches wide would separate them. By reaching in to the planting soil and always walking in the aisles, the gardener would keep the soil loose and friable, so no heavy digging would be necessary after the first time. Since all the growing soil is contained within the growing squares, that soil could be improved while the soil in the aisles would be left unimproved.

By planting in individual square feet within the garden squares, all of the wasted space of single row gardening is eliminated so that a square foot garden takes up only 20 percent of the space of a conventional garden. This major accomplishment eliminated 80 percent of the work and expense of a conventional garden.

Each garden square is divided in half each way, then again in half each way, thus forming sixteen square feet. This can be done by laying down sticks or string, or just marking the soil with a stick. Then each individual square foot is planted, often each with a different crop.

Since each square foot is such a small space, we can afford to improve the original soil all at once by adding peat moss, compost, vermiculite, and well-rotted manure to make it the perfect soil, even if our natural soil is clay, or hard and rocky. If we want to eliminate all the work, we can afford to use a packaged premixed soil. Either of these steps will satisfy the plant's first requirement, to have a perfect soil.

This same square foot, when divided in half each way, forms four six-inch squares, each perfect for a head of leaf lettuce. Thus requirement number two—adequate growing space—is met.

Because our garden takes up so little space, we now have time to pick any weeds as soon as they're seen, or we can easily cover the square bed with a chicken wire cage, if rabbits are a problem. That fulfills requirement number three.

The same applies to requirement number four. It's far easier to find a sunny spot for a small garden, and chances are that spot can be closer to the house, where you'll notice the garden more often and take better care of it. Watering is done by ladling from a bucket, and, because of the saucer-shaped depression around each plant and the large amount of humus in the soil, your plants will get plenty of moisture.

Continuous Harvest

And what does the home gardener get? Well, you can get your continuous harvest in two ways, by planting every square foot with a different crop or by planting the same crop in succession.

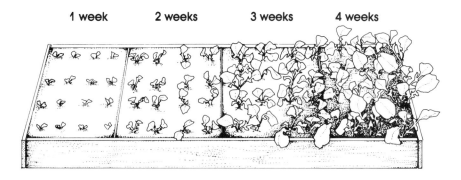

By planting a new square foot of radishes each week, the home gardener can have a weekly supply of 16 radishes.

For example, a square foot of sixteen radishes can be planted every week, resulting in a small but continuous weekly harvest. And, because of the tremendous size reduction in your garden, your labor is greatly reduced. Size is down 80 percent, but labor is down even more, as much as 90 percent. Weeding is quick and easy, and watering becomes fun. You're so close to your plants that you can see any problems when they first develop. And by planting your home garden with lots of square feet of flowers and herbs—yes, mix them in together—you'll have the most attractive garden imaginable. Since it's so easy to care for, it will stay weed-free and be continually productive.

Other Advantages

You'll see other advantages as you work with the square foot system. You won't need yardsticks or fancy measuring devices. When you lay out your garden in four-foot squares, protecting your plants becomes simple. Wire-covered wood frames, four feet square, can be used as cages for protection from pests and the weather. They can be moved about the garden quickly and easily.

It's easy to move even the larger frame for the commercial square foot garden.

Square foot gardening is very practical and easy to adapt to any situation or location, whether it be patio, rooftop, or a garden for the handicapped. For the latter, you can build planter boxes of any size by adding a plywood bottom, then raise them for a gardener confined to a wheelchair or for those who can't bend over. Even children, who usually lose interest in gardening, love the square foot system because long, tedious hours of work aren't necessary.

For sit-down or stand-up gardening, drill drainage holes in a 4 X 4-foot plywood sheet, add 1 X 6-inch lumber sides, fill with a rich planting mix.

Well, that's it in a nutshell. The system is so simple that people keep asking me why no one else ever thought of it. All I can say is that the experts and horticulturally trained people must be too close to their subject. Colleges are still teaching single row gardening because they're geared more to farming and commercial agriculture, and everyone assumes that home gardening is just a small-scale version of farming. Besides, most people don't stop to question why we do something if it's always been done that way. They just go along with it because they think it must be correct.

Let's look at square foot gardening in more detail. First we'll review the basic system, then we will see how easily it can be adapted to a productive and profitable cash garden.

When to Work

The first question many ask is when is the best time to prepare the beds. If you are the very organized type of person that plans well ahead, fall is the best time and spring is the worst. That's because you shouldn't work the soil when it's wet and cold. But how many of us are that well organized? When you decide you want a cash garden, you want it right then. So go ahead at any time of the year as long as the soil isn't frozen or so muddy that when you squeeze a handful, water drips out and it's perfect for making mud pies. If it's that bad, cover the squares with clear plastic to let the sun in and keep the rain out, and soon the soil can be worked.

The Garden Layout

A square foot garden is composed of any number of four-foot square planting areas. Each area can be bordered with string, wood, railroad ties, bricks, or anything you can think of. Putting a border around each garden block helps to define it and keeps visitors from walking in the garden soil.

I recommend building wood sides out of one-by-fours or two-by-sixes, almost any size you can get your hands on. It's usually free for the asking, particularly if you're near a construction site. Builders throw out tons of wood. They will be glad to let you take it if you ask. Look for any house construction in your neighborhood. You can also use old lumber, or you can, as a last resort, buy it.

Should it be treated? My answer to this is, "Only if you can afford it." If you can't get pressure-treated lumber, I wouldn't bother to paint it with a preservative.

The Perfect Soil

One of the key elements in the success of your square foot garden is providing the perfect soil mix. If you provide this attractive medium, your plants will grow twice as fast as in the usual garden soil.

The perfect soil is filled with humus, organic material that acts like tiny sponges. Peat moss, vermiculite, and compost and well-rotted manure all do the same job. They allow the soil to drain because they're separated by many open spaces, and yet, because they act like sponges, they hold the moisture, not the water. The moisture is held in each little particle, and the roots of the plants grow around each particle in the soil. When they need moisture, they suck it up. Nutrients as well as moisture are held in these particles of humus, and the plant roots can take them up as they are needed.

This is very different from conventional soil which, if it's sandy, has many open spaces and drains too quickly, with no moisture being retained, or, if it's very clayey, becomes waterlogged. Many soils around the country are clay, and they either become as hard as concrete when dry, and no water can sink into them, or when they finally get saturated, no air spaces are left, so the plant roots suffer again.

The perfect soil is very humusy, loose, and not compacted, well-drained, friable, easily dug, and full of earthworms, a sure sign that the humus content is high. If you have this perfect soil, you'll get ideal growth from your plants. They won't experience water stress, a result of the plants getting too much or too little water, which affects their growth and production, and the taste of the harvest, which is most important for a cash garden.

Creating the Soil

How do you create this perfect soil? The easiest and quickest method is to buy bags of planting mix. Make sure the bag says MIX on it. Don't buy the inexpensive, on-sale potting soil, or black dirt, or something like that.

Blended planting mixes are expensive, but they will last you a lifetime. You can take a cue from the commercial growers. They don't mix their own soil anymore; they buy bags of prepared mix, which is almost a perfect blend. It is composed mostly of peat moss and vermiculite. Some mixes have trace elements and basic fertilizer. They've been adjusted for the correct pH for growing plants. Some have ground-up bark, a little perlite, and occasionally a little bit of sand.

You can improve these soil mixes by adding homemade compost, thus increasing the amount of organic matter. Before you loosen your existing soil, test it for pH, and add lime or sulfur, depending on the results, to bring the pH within the desired 6 to 7 range, which is slightly acid. Most vegetables do quite well in that range. Then add a little bit of fertilizer, about one pound of 5-10-5 to each four-by-four-foot area.

Now dig and loosen your existing soil. How deep? Only as deep as you are comfortable working. Don't go extra deep and hurt your back for the sake of saying you went down twelve inches. The plants will hardly know the difference. They're going to be so happy with the perfect soil mix you're going to add on top that they'll do just fine.

Remove any sticks, stones, or roots, and break up the large clods. Then add a layer of your packaged or homemade soil mix, some three or four inches of it. Turn it under and mix it well with the original soil. Remember to avoid stepping on this soil, even when working it into shape. Always work from the outside of the garden squares. Wood borders help to remind you to stay off the soil.

If your new planting mix is packed in a bag or bale, it's best to moisten it ahead of time. There is nothing worse than very dry, powdery peat moss and vermiculite. It blows all over. So, a day or two before you're going to use it, poke a hole in the bag, insert a hose and let it run slowly for five or ten minutes. The soil will become uniformly moist and easy to handle.

Borders

The height of a wooden border around the blocks depends a lot on the quality of your soil. If your soil is terrible—and it seems everyone complains about that—don't even worry about it. Build your garden up, starting from the surface of the ground. Make your wooden border at least six inches high and fill it with the perfect soil mix.

The planting blocks can be laid out in any configuration that fits your yard and landscaping. Keep in mind that you will add vertical frames on the north side for all those tomatoes, cucumbers, and melons you want to grow.

Adding dividers to your four-foot squares to show individual square feet looks nice and helps remind you of the spacing. It's also easier this way to keep the plants in exactly the right place in relation to each other. To divide them, lay down four-foot sticks or staple string to the wooden sides. A better material that won't rot is inexpensive plastic clothesline.

Paths

Paths between your squares can be any width, from one foot to three or four feet, depending on the space you have available. The surface of these paths can be anything that fits in with your garden style, the looks of your yard, and your budget. It can be plain soil (run an action hoe over it once a week to eliminate the weeds), a hay mulch, wood chips, or chopped leaves. You can lay down boards and walk on them. Some just leave grass, as long as the aisles are wide enough to be mowed. You can even put in stone to make it very decorative. Keep in mind ease of maintenance and looks before you decide what you want.

EFFECT OF AISLE WIDTH ON EFFICIENT USE OF SPACE

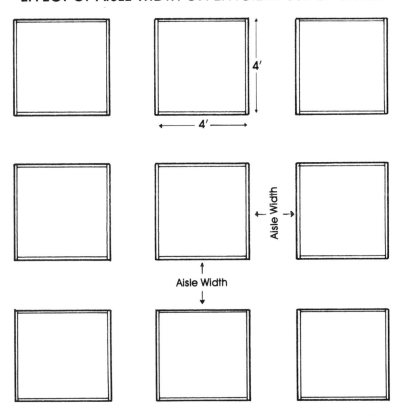

If you're going to have nine 4'x4' (16 square feet) planting squares, here's how aisles of different widths would affect the percentage of your overall garden space devoted to growing.

Aisle Width	Growing Space/ Garden Space	Efficiency of Space Used
12"	16 sq. ft. x 9=144 sq. ft. 14' x 14'=196 sq. ft.	144/196=73%
18"	16 sq. ft. x 9=144 sq. ft. 15' x 15'=225 sq. ft.	144/225=64%
24"	16 sq. ft. x 9=144 sq. ft. 16' x 16'=256 sq. ft.	144/256=56%

As the aisles become wider, the proportion of the space devoted to production decreases rapidly. You should find a balance between comfort and efficiency that suits your situation.

If you have limited space for a garden, or want to have the most efficient layout, the width of the aisles is important. But since you're not improving the soil in the aisles, the main effect will be on ease of use and attractiveness.

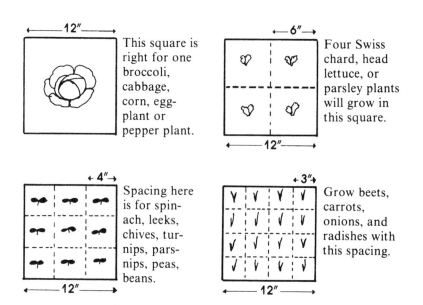

This square is right for one broccoli, cabbage, corn, eggplant or pepper plant.

Four Swiss chard, head lettuce, or parsley plants will grow in this square.

Spacing here is for spinach, leeks, chives, turnips, parsnips, peas, beans.

Grow beets, carrots, onions, and radishes with this spacing.

Plant Spacing

Plants can be divided into four easily remembered sizes. I think of them in terms of shirt sizes: extra large, large, medium, and small.

Extra large plants go one per square foot. Plant them in the middle of that square foot, in a saucer-shaped depression.

Large plants go four per square foot. Use your finger to trace two lines in the soil, dividing that square foot in half each way to get four spaces.

Medium plants go nine per square foot. Divide the space into thirds each way and you'll have nine squares.

Small plants go sixteen per square foot. This is just as easy to divide. Divide the square in half each way, then take two fingers, spread them apart about three inches, and poke four holes in each quarter of your square foot.

No rulers, no measuring, no division, no mathematics—you can do all your spacing by eye. The nicest part is that if you make a mistake, you can rub out your marks with your hand and start all over again.

Templates

Many people have designed templates or other devices to help them in spacing their plants. You don't really need them, but it adds a little fun to gardening.

In the cash garden, since you're planting more than just one foot at a time, you can build a small frame that will fit across one bed. Use molding, then staple string across to indicate the divisions. If you build two such frames, divide one with string to give a division every six inches (four plants per square foot), the other every four inches (nine plants per square foot). That makes it very quick and easy when you're doing a lot of planting, which you will be doing in the cash system. You just lay the frame down on the bed, poke your holes in the center of each space, and drop in the seeds or plants.

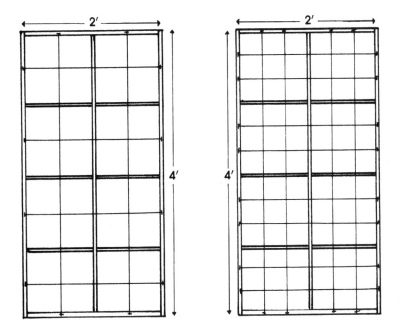

Make these templates for quick and easy planting. The one at left divides each square foot into four spaces; the one at right divides it into nine spaces.

Another handy spacing material is wire fencing. It comes with many size openings, including six-inch and four-inch squares. By applying a little spray paint to sections of the fencing, you can indicate twelve-inch squares, and the subdivisions will be the wire itself. Sometimes you can cut a few wires to give just the right spacing. This can be done for an individual square foot, or for an entire one-by-four-foot area. The fencing is self-supporting and needs no frame.

Those who are planning a large garden may want to make these spacing devices two by two feet, or even four feet square. These are harder to handle, though. The smaller ones are probably all you need for any size garden, because they are so simple to lift and move.

These spacing devices can be hung from nails on the garage walls. In order to make sure they don't disappear in the garden, paint the frames with bright colors, just as you do tool handles.

Too Crowded?

Many people, especially those accustomed to seeing wide spaces between garden rows, believe the spacing in a square foot garden must be too crowded. However, they are overlooking one important factor. When you provide the perfect soil mix, moisture and nutrients will be available to your plants at all times. This means that the roots won't have to spread out looking for these essentials. Thus, your spacing can be as compact as possible, as we have it in the square foot system. We don't crowd the plants but we don't waste any space, either.

Watering

Plants do best when they have a continuous supply of moisture. Notice that I didn't say water. There's a big difference between water and moisture in the soil. If your soil is filled with water, it plugs up all of the open air spaces, driving out the oxygen. The roots will suffer if this condition remains too long. Of course, with your perfect soil mix, this won't happen, because all of the excess water will drain away, yet all the organic matter or humus in the soil will retain moisture, allowing the plant roots to take it up when it's needed.

WATERING TIPS

- Use the cup and bucket method for maximum efficiency.

- Always have a few buckets of water sitting in the sun to warm up.

- Install shutoff connectors at end of hose.

- Never water from overhead by using a sprinkler or hand-held hose.

- Water the soil root area, not the plant tops.

- Plant in a shallow saucer depression to eliminate runoff and waste.

- Water in the morning or late afternoon, not the evening.

- Spray seed plantings daily. Don't allow the surface soil to dry.

- When filling your buckets, lay an extra length of hose coiled up in the sun so the water will warm. (Watch out—it can get too hot.)

Watering the square foot garden is very simple. The system recognizes that plants do better with warm rather than cold water. This is particularly true if you're adding a water-soluble fertilizer. The nutrients dissolve much faster in warm water and are more readily available.

The easiest way to water is to let several large pails of water stand in the sun to warm. Ladle out one to three cups of this water for each plant. Using this method, you get closer to your plants. You see how they're growing, whether they're ready for harvest, if any bugs are bothering them, and whether the plants are growing well. How many times have you gone into your garden and found the beans overgrown and no longer producing, or filled with bugs and beyond saving? Watering this way, you'll notice early on when a plant needs help.

How often you water depends on how dry the soil is, the weather, the time of year, and your area of the country. In general, you'll have to water at least once a week, and probably twice during warmer weather. In southern parts of the country, you'll have to water three times a week. Transplants should be watered lightly almost every day, at least until they start growing. You can usually tell they're growing from the color and the erectness of the leaves. You'll also see new green growth starting as soon as the roots have acclimated themselves to the soil.

Bill Kulkman's eggplants grow up through the mesh and need no other support.

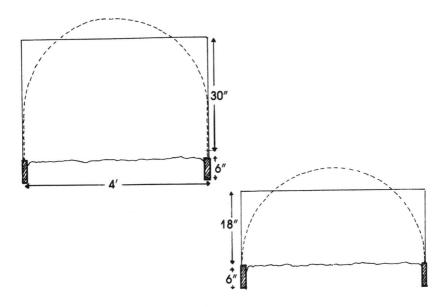

To make these supports, 8 feet of fencing is needed for the 18-inch support, 10 feet for the 30-inch support. Arch the support for weather protection, bend it flat across the top for plant support.

Supporting the Plants

While you're watering you'll notice whether your plants are getting large enough to need support. Since your soil is so loose and easily worked, the plants will be less able to support themselves than they would in poor, heavy soil. This is not a disadvantage, it just means that you have to provide support. The square foot support is easy and practical to install, particularly if you have wooden borders. You use the same wire fencing you used for your spacing devices. Choose one with openings you can put your hand through. Tack it to one border board, arch it over your plants, and nail it to the board on the opposite side. The openings in the fencing will be large enough to allow you to reach through to work on the plants, which can grow up through the mesh. You'll never again have to worry about finding your pepper plants blown over after a heavy storm. The wire fencing must be put on when the plants are about half grown, before they need the support.

This same wire framework, only a little higher, can be used as a support for all sorts of garden protectors. For example, in early spring, you can attach clear plastic to the frame with clothespins and you'll have a miniature greenhouse.

In the summer you'll do just the opposite. You'll cover the wire frame with shade cloth to protect your plants from extreme heat. Using this method, you'll be able to grow lettuce through the entire summer in just about any part of the country. It's even done in Florida.

If you have a very wet, cold snap, you might want to throw on that plastic cover again to keep out heavy rains. This way you can extend the beginning and end of the growing season several weeks with very little work.

Your wire framework can also be used as a safeguard against pests. By substituting one-inch chicken wire, you can keep out the rabbits.

By making the frame a bit differently, you can move it from one area to another. Rather than attaching the wire to your garden frames, you can make a frame out of smaller wood, say one-by-twos or molding, staple the wire onto the frame, and then use it as a

When transplanting in hot, sunny weather, add a shade cloth to the wire frame, and leave it in place for a few days.

moveable device. Transplants, when they are first taken out into the garden, must be protected from sun and hot, dry winds. It's so easy, once you've planted an area, to move a frame over it and cover the wire with shade cloth.

The plants can still get air through the sides, so it won't get too hot inside, but the frame keeps the wind off the plants. After a few days, you can move the frame to another area. In a large, single row garden, when transplants are set out, they go into shock and appear wilted and almost dead. Although they usually recover, this setback will affect the harvest. Using the square foot spacing and a shade frame will allow your plants to get off to a quick, easy, and healthy start.

Starting Seeds

In order to have a continuous harvest, you will plant on a continuous schedule. But it's very easy. Remember, you're only planting a few square feet at a time. If you have transplants ready, it's very easy to put them in, then give them a drink of water and a little shade. You can either purchase the transplants or start them yourself, and I've developed a seed starting method that is very simple and easy.

As an example, if you want a continuous supply of leaf lettuce, you should plant seeds every week. To have several varieties, start a different variety every other week.

Use inexpensive containers such as margarine cups. Wash and dry them, then drill four drain holes through a stack of them, using an electric drill with a quarter-inch bit.

Fill them with coarse vermiculite, sprinkle on a few seeds, and cover them with a thin layer of vermiculite. Set the cups in a pan with about a half-inch of warm water. The vermiculite will soak up the water and keep the seeds just moist enough to sprout. Label each container and keep the pan in a place where the temperature is about 70° F. around the clock.

When the first sprout appears, put the container into strong sunlight or under a fluorescent light.

Maintaining constant temperature is no longer important. It can drop at night. The roots can be kept moist by keeping the cups in a pan or tray with about a quarter-inch of water in it.

Drill holes in margarine cups, fill them with vermiculite, and set them in a shallow pan with a little 70-degree water in the bottom. Keep it at that level to keep the vermiculite moist.

When you start your seeds, the temperature of about 70° F. is important. Light is not important at this point, but the minute those seeds start to sprout, the cups must be put in full sunlight. The only other important factor is moisture. The vermiculite must be constantly moist, but not sopping wet. Never submerge the cups. Just set them in a shallow pan or tray of water so they can take up moisture constantly.

Transplanting

As soon as the seeds are up, they should be transplanted into four-packs or individual containers. *Do not wait until the second set of leaves branches out,* as is recommended in all the garden books. That is much too late. The plants will become rootbound and will go into deep shock when they are transplanted.

Depending on the dexterity of your fingers, transplant them just as soon as you can safely handle them. This is done by digging around the plant with the pointed end of a pencil while holding onto one of the tiny leaves with your fingers. Lift it carefully. If you can take some of the vermiculite clinging to the roots, that is preferable, but not critical.

Have your containers ready, filled with a good quality, moist potting soil mix. Do not tamp it down, but settle it by tapping the containers lightly on the table. With your pencil, poke a hole large and deep enough so the roots of the seedling don't touch the sides. Carefully lower the seedling into the hole. Don't stuff the roots in or let them hang out the sides. They should extend all the way down into the hole. Then gently fill in the hole with your pencil.

Arrange the containers in a tray with a small amount of water in the bottom and place them in the shade for at least a day or two. Once the plants are over the shock of transplanting, they can be brought out into the light, and perhaps on the third day back into full sunlight. Do not leave them in darkness or they will try to grow towards the light and will get very leggy by the end of three or four days.

Remember, your little seedlings are still babies: they need care and protection from the sun and wind, from extreme hot and cold temperatures, and from pests. They need warmth and moisture. Keep a little bit of water in their tray and use a good potting soil mix, which will suck up that moisture.

Growing Transplants

Your next project is to grow those seedlings into good-sized transplants.

If they have been growing for more than two weeks in the same container, you might add a liquid fertilizer to the water, particularly if they are the "leaf" type of plant, which needs extra nitrogen.

Don't keep them in these containers too long or they will become rootbound. The standard six-packs will encourage the plant roots to grow round and round, eventually becoming rootbound.

Styrofoam containers with pyramid-shaped holes and open bottoms offer one solution. These are sometimes called speedling trays. When they are suspended in air, so that light and air can get underneath the container, the roots will be pruned by the light. They won't grow out into the light and dangle from the container, but will stop growing out and branch out higher up. This promotes extremely strong root growth in the plant, which will transplant very easily.

These containers can also be watered from underneath by setting them in a tray filled with water for a couple of hours. Then they must be taken out, or the roots will grow out into the water, eliminating the big advantage of this type of container.

Transplants can be raised outdoors in warmer weather. If you don't have a greenhouse, you can set up a nursery area with one of the wire frame covers and have plenty of transplants ready to go in the garden every week.

Assure a continuous harvest by always having seedlings ready to plant.

After transplanting, if it's early spring or late fall or you're having heavy rains, put a plastic-covered wire frame over the transplants. This will let in lots of light and air, but will keep the heavy rains off the tender plants. It will also protect them from rabbits and deer and anything that wants to nibble on them.

When setting out transplants, use the "cup and saucer" method. Form a shallow depression around the plant as you set it in the ground. This allows water to seep down to the roots. Water immediately after transplanting. Some people like to use a manure tea or a weak solution of water-soluble fertilizer.

The next thing you should do, particularly if the sun is going to be out that day or the next, is to provide a wire frame shade cover.

The best time of day to transplant is whatever time you have available. With the square foot system, it's no longer critical to wait until sundown or to start early in the morning. By providing the shade cover and watering immediately, you can transplant at any time of the day, at your convenience.

Sowing in the Garden

What about those vegetables that are sown directly in the garden. These include the root crops—radishes, beets, and carrots—and vegetables such as corn and beans. Here the procedure is even easier. You divide each square foot either in half or thirds each way.

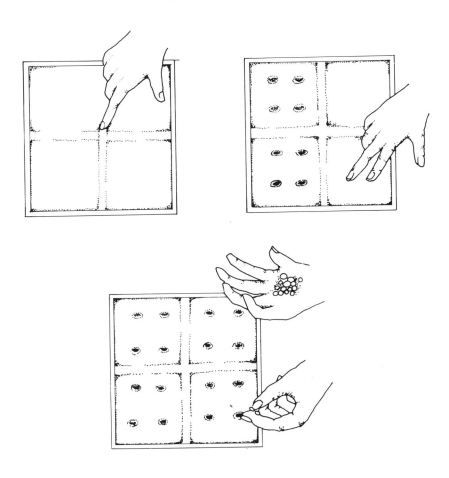

Then you make the holes and drop in a pinch of seeds. How many in a pinch? Two or three. Cover with soil and water with a fine spray watering can.

Snip off Extras

Most of them will sprout, and you don't want them to crowd each other. The minute they're up, use scissors to snip off the extra ones, leaving just one per hole. That way there'll be no crowding, and you'll have no trouble distinguishing your plants from any weeds that come up.

Cut, don't pull up, extra seedlings, to avoid damaging other seedlings.

If you see any weeds, pull them up with two fingers. This gives all your plants a much better start, and, again, they will grow much faster than in a single row garden.

Harvesting

One of the biggest advantages to square foot gardening is that the minute you harvest each square foot, you can prepare the soil and replant it. This gives you a continuous crop, and in many parts of the country you can replant the same square foot four or five times per year.

Harvesting is also done a little differently than in a conventional garden. You don't have to overplant in order to ensure a large harvest of every item at all times.

I like to think that the square foot system is more adaptable to our modern way of life. We get out to the garden about every day to see what's ready. We harvest it, and then we plan our meal around that. It's like going to a salad bar in a restaurant. Rather than ordering a side dish or a certain salad, you select what appeals to you, and that becomes your meal. By picking whatever is ready, you harvest it at its peak, its perfect taste and perfect size.

Since we're attuned today to eating more vegetables raw, it becomes even easier to have a variety of raw vegetables from the garden in a salad or as an appetizer.

Cooked vegetables can be either a main dish or a side dish. You can even pickle several vegetables and serve them as an appetizer the next evening. Or eat them as a snack—what could be better for the health of you and your family than to munch on fresh vegetables rather than junk food? You might even get to like them a little better when the harvest varies from day to day, instead of having the same old thing for weeks on end.

Another advantage of this system is that plants harvested before they reach full size don't need as much room to grow. For example, Swiss chard. Many people who read about putting four plants in one square foot, knowing how huge some of those plants can grow, immediately assume they're crowded and won't do well.

One method of harvesting Swiss chard is to keep cutting the outer leaves.

If they harvest continuously by cutting off the outer leaves on the stalks, they will find that the plants do very well indeed in the space of four per square foot.

The same is true of parsley. One square foot of parsley usually produces all that a family can eat, and if you harvest continuously, it produces all spring, summer, and fall. When the cold weather sets in, you can dig up your parsley plants, put them in pots, and move them indoors to become houseplants that will produce all winter.

Harvesting under the cash system is a little different, but only because we're looking for more volume. Under that system we might harvest the entire plant of Swiss chard by cutting off all of the leaves, including the medium and smaller ones. We just have to leave the center of the plant still growing so more shoots will come out. More on this in a later chapter.

Replanting

With vegetables that are harvested only once, such as radishes and carrots, you'll replant each square foot as soon as you've completed the harvest.

You do this by:

1. Adding a trowelful of compost, manure, or peat moss and a light sprinkling of fertilizer, either 5-10-5 or a prepared balanced organic mix.

2. Turning the square over with a trowel. Remember, the soil has remained very loose and friable because you never walked on it.

3. Smoothing it out with your hands.

4. Deciding what you're going to plant next.

5. Popping in either seeds or transplants, and watering them.

And that's it. You're all done. It couldn't be simpler, and yet you've harvested, rotated the crops, improved the soil, and made a succession planting, all in a matter of a few minutes. You didn't write out any charts, or study anything, and yet you did all those good things without even thinking about them, because the square foot gardening system is so automatic and so foolproof.

A large mesh makes it easy to harvest tomatoes grown on it.

Vertical Gardening

People ask me, "Sure, that sounds good for small salad crops, but what about the big, rambling plants like tomatoes and cucumbers?"

Well, they're all grown vertically in the square foot system. Vertical gardening saves twice as much space as the regular square foot garden. The basic theory is that all vine crops, which tend to spread out, can be trained to go up.

There are other reasons why vertical gardening works so well. It's far easier to prepare the soil and water the plants. You have to prepare only one square foot for a tomato plant.

And, finally, you can harvest standing up, with little bending over. That saves the old back.

To use this method, you need a support to hold up the plant, and that's easy to supply. Your frames must be strong and able to hold up all those tomatoes you are going to grow.

Cucumber and tomato plants, when fully grown and six feet tall, have a lot of leaves and fruit. By early fall, when we start getting heavy rains and winds, your frames and the plants are like sails on a boat, so the frames must be very strong. That's why I selected steel posts or pipe. If you feel that you have to provide additional support, tie guy wires to them. Vertical frames can be attached to your planter boxes to provide additional support, as long as the frames are on the north side so they don't shade other plants.

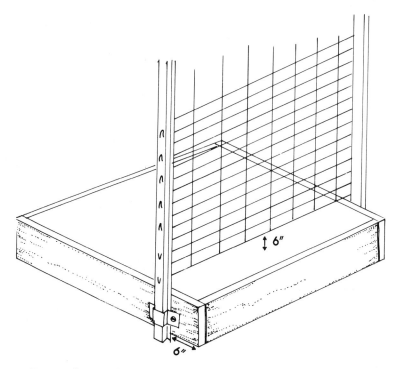

Locate frame 6 inches in from box end, and start the wire mesh about 6 inches above the soil level.

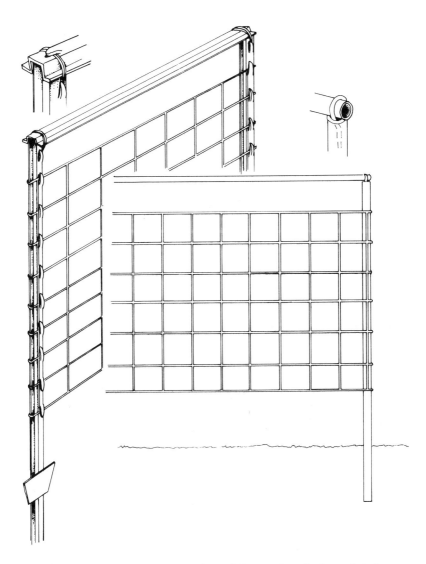

Use steel fence posts, left, water pipe, right, or electrical conduit for supports. Cut a 5½-foot section of 4-foot tomato growing wire to hang between the supports.

To make a frame, use either steel fence posts, threaded, galvanized water pipe, or half-inch, thin wall type electrical conduit with slip fittings. You can buy these either new at a plumbing or electrical supply house or you can find some used at a junkyard.

Make the frame seven feet tall (one foot of that will be in the ground) and four feet wide. If pounding these into the ground will be a problem, plan on two-foot legs that can be pounded into the soil, and five-foot additions. If you use the conduit, bend it with a pipe bender, to avoid kinking and breaking the pipe.

Cover the framework with tomato wire with six-by-four-inch openings (it's sold by the roll in most hardware stores) so the plants can be easily woven in and out of the openings and you can reach through to prune or harvest. Don't put up chicken wire, concrete reinforcing wire, or small-spaced netting. It will lead to a lot of problems later. The plants will not burn on the wire, as has often been thought, and I like to use wire because it doesn't stretch or sag.

Some people put up vertical supports and then weave string back and forth. This is a very tedious procedure, and their frames end up looking terrible at the end of the season.

Your structures can be any height, depending on their strength. The plants will grow quite tall. If you have fairly hard soil and you're going to pound pipe into the ground and tamp around it very hard, you can build your structures six feet tall. The plants will easily grow to that height, and they'll bear fruit right to the top. In fact, in most parts of the country they'll grow up and over the top, and you'll wonder what to do next. You can trim the ends of the plants, which won't hurt them and it will force all the fruit to ripen faster. Or you can let the plants drape over the top and start down the other side.

Any vine crop can be grown this way. That includes tomatoes, cucumbers, pole beans, winter squash, and all kinds of melons, even watermelons. Many melon varieties today weigh under ten pounds, and I've found that they hang on the vine without support.

With vertical gardening, you'll be planting four square feet at once, on the north side of a garden square. To make watering easy, scoop out a shallow depression or trench along that four-foot length. Then plant all of your plants into this trench at the proper spacing, and you'll find that watering suddenly becomes very easy. You won't waste a single drop of water, and it will go right down to the roots. An ideal watering method is to lay an irrigation hose or a drip irrigation system along the trench.

Some plants, such as cucumbers and melons, will climb by themselves. Tomatoes and squash have to be helped a bit. Weave the top of the main stem in and out of the large wire openings once a week.

Weave your tomato vines in and out of the mesh.

In order to achieve the maximum production in the smallest space, prune tomatoes to a single or double stem. This means cutting off all side branches—suckers, as they're commonly called— thereby forcing more energy into the main stem where the fruit will be able to draw on it for development.

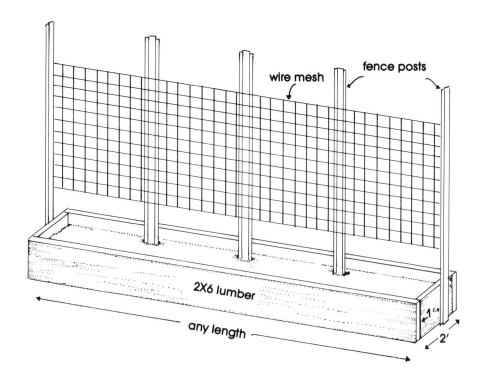

This garden can be used for tomatoes, cucumbers, and other crops.

Many people use the vertical garden as a visual border or divider. It can be used as a screen, so you can't see your neighbors behind it, or the dog pens or garbage pails or whatever you want to hide. Or you could put up entire rows of fencing spaced three feet apart and have a separate vertical garden. It all depends on how many vine crops you want to grow. If it's just a few, you can locate your vertical frames along the north side of the garden blocks. In effect, you will be planting vine crops in the last four square feet of the garden beds. These vines will climb up the frame, and the remaining square feet in each one of those beds will be planted in non-vine crops.

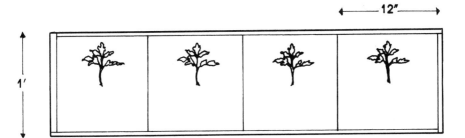

Tomatoes, squash, and muskmelons require a square foot per plant.

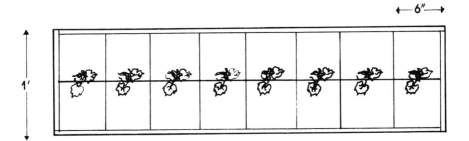

Set cucumber plants six inches apart in vertical gardening.

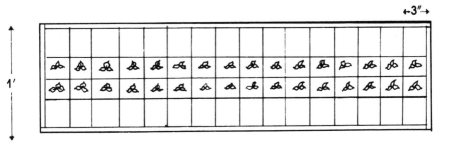

A double row of peas or pole beans can be planted this way.

Cash Gardening Adaptations

Someone starting a cash gardening business will want a much larger garden than the eight to twelve blocks of a typical family garden. And they will want to get the maximum growing space out of their backyard.

For them, we will place those four-by-four boxes together end to end, thus creating a four-foot-wide garden bed of any convenient length. You can still reach in from both sides, because you'll have narrow aisles in between each long bed.

In the past, I've never recommended this, because the minute people see a long bed, they start picturing individual rows running the length of it. Before you know it, they're right back where they started, thinking in terms of a single row garden, even though it's on a raised bed.

By having crops in all stages of growth, there's always a harvest ready.

But we want to get the maximum growing space available and are usually willing to give up the convenience of being able to walk around each growing area. Now we have to walk around a larger area, four feet by twelve feet, for example, but this will give us about 10 percent more growing space with little inconvenience.

The advantages or special adaptations of this bed layout for your cash garden are particularly evident if you live where you have a very short season, a very hot, dry climate, or a very cool, wet growing season. It even has great advantages if you live in the South and have mild winters. With wooden sides on your beds and the proper wire covers, it's possible to grow crops such as lettuce, parsley, and spinach right through ten to eleven months of the year. Think back to the wooden sides and the method of making wire enclosures, then throwing on anything from clear plastic to shade film to chicken wire, to keep out the sun, heavy rains, rabbits, or whatever else might bother your plants.

Long Frame?

Some people, seeing a long bed, consider building a long frame that will hold a cloche or continuous arch cover. This is not advisable, because it's difficult for one person to handle it. If you think in terms of four-by-four areas, you can readily move any of your covers from one area to another.

You can see that the square foot system is easily adaptable to any conditions and any area of the country. People write and say, "We live in Arizona. Please give us the special requirements for our area." Well, there aren't any. A plant's requirements are the same, no matter what the area, and the same devices can be used. You just use them at a different time of the year and in a slightly different manner. And, since everyone in the country thinks he has the worst possible soil, the square foot gardening mix will solve all kinds of soil problems, whether it's Georgia red clay, Louisiana gumbo, or California sand.

Square foot gardening is a totally new method with new ideas, and requires that you adopt some new ways of thinking. But everyone can get used to them once they learn the basic system. Then it's just a matter of adapting all the basic square foot gardening ideas to their particular yard, climate, and growing conditions.

At first I thought there might be a lot of adaptation necessary for a cash garden. But aside from placing the squares end to end to eliminate one aisle, there really aren't any special or different things to do.

Of course, you're going to want a much larger harvest for cash than for family, but all that means is you will be planting four or six square feet of radishes every week, rather than just one, or sixteen to thirty-two square feet of peppers instead of just six or eight square feet.

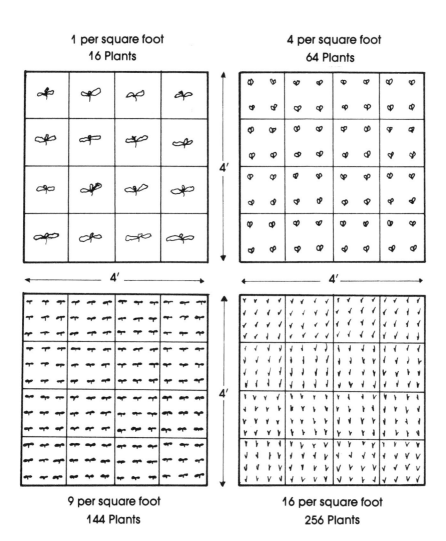

1 per square foot
16 Plants

4 per square foot
64 Plants

4'

4'

4'

4'

9 per square foot
144 Plants

16 per square foot
256 Plants

Once you get started you'll see that even keeping records is very simple. If you want to harvest twelve or fourteen heads of cos (romaine) lettuce every week, you'll need to start about twenty-five to thirty seeds weekly, pot up about twenty seedlings, and transplant sixteen of the best plants into four square feet of garden space. Each step happens weekly, so you have a production line going. Since the lettuce will take about six weeks to mature, you'll need six weeks of garden space, or six times four square feet reserved for cos lettuce.

That's all there is to it. It's really very easy and it about runs itself. No need to draw up very complicated plans or diagrams. Just establish the base amount of each vegetable and keep planting, growing, and harvesting.

Chapter 4

Your Market

$ If your square foot garden business is to be a success, you must find the perfect market for your produce.

The time and effort you spend searching out and securing a market before you start will pay higher dividends than any other thing you can do. If people starting a new business would spend more time investigating where and how they're going to sell and who's going to buy, the failure rate (five out of ten fail in the first year) would be cut in half.

Aim for sales that are:

1. Continuous.

2. Assured, if not guaranteed.

3. Prompt, well-paying, and profitable for your investment of time and money.

How often I have heard, "After business picks up and we sell more items, our costs will come down so we can make a profit." Often it never happens. You must make a profit right from the start.

Or I hear, "We're selling a lot but on large orders we have to give big discounts, and now we're having trouble collecting."

Avoid the Headaches

Collections and cash flow are two of the biggest headaches in any business, large or small, part- or full-time. Ask anyone in business. It's enough to discourage the strongest of heart and the most eager beginner.

So what does all this mean to you, who just want to earn a little extra money? It means you should start in the right business, find the best market, and then sell the right product in the most profitable way. If you were going to sell your grandmother's homemade soup, you could sell it from your porch, door-to-door, or at the local farmers' market. Or you could open a small store, sell it through local stores, or get a large chain or national store to carry it.

Marketing your vegetables is no different. First you have to decide *how* you will sell them. You have your choice of selling at wholesale or retail. Wholesale means you get only half of the retail price, but you sell in large quantities—ten crates of lettuce at a time rather than by the head, as in retail. One advantage of wholesaling is dealing with fewer customers. The disadvantage is your vulnerability when relying on just a few customers and the consequences if you lose them.

The second thing to consider is the time you want to spend producing your product against the time you want to spend selling it. This depends a lot on each individual. Do you prefer to be with people or by yourself? Do you like to meet people and chat? Are you a talker or a listener? It make a big difference, because in one type of produce business you'll spend 75 percent of your time selling and 25 percent growing, while another type will have you in the garden 75 percent of the time and only 25 percent of the time in the marketplace.

Another consideration is how successful you want to be and how much money you want to make. Be honest with yourself. Everyone says, "I want to make a lot of money—as much as possible," but what is meant is, "I'd like to have something to do to keep me busy. If I can make a profit, all the better." They may want to work in the garden and have a market for their labor, or they may want to talk to people all day. We're all lonely at times and need companionship.

By asking yourself the following questions, you can get a good idea of the success potential of a new business:

1. Does it take little money or effort to get started?

2. Will I find the work enjoyable, and does it lie within my capabilities?

3. Can it be run at a time that's convenient?

4. Is there little or no competition, so my product can command top dollar?

5. Will I have customers or sales lined up ahead of time?

6. Can I collect in cash at the time of sale?

7. Will I be assured of continuous sales?

8. Can I sell all I make or produce?

9. Can I sell at retail, so I can get top price?

10. Can I increase or decrease production without affecting my market?

If you ask all ten of the above questions about the square foot cash gardening business, you will get affirmative answers.

There are two parts to most businesses: production and sales. First let's look at production as it relates to the ten questions.

1. You'll be using your backyard and your own tools: no major investment needed.

2. If you enjoy gardening, you're ready for business. If you don't, don't start.

3. Nothing in gardening requires you to open the gate at 9 A.M. or even to be there every day. You can garden whenever you like, as long as the work gets done.

4. If you live anywhere except in the middle of a truck farm, you're all set.

5-10. All part of sales.

Notice that six of the above are related to sales. Now let's look at the different aspects of sales—where, when, how, and who.

Where to Sell Your Produce

First, let's look at the retail possibilities.

1. **Your Neighborhood.** Let neighbors stop by, or you take orders and deliver. You'll be able to make cash sales and get top dollar for your product. A side benefit is that you'll be able to visit with friends. The drawbacks are that you probably won't do much volume and there'll be no guarantee of continuous sales. Because of this, you won't sell out every day, and there will be some waste.

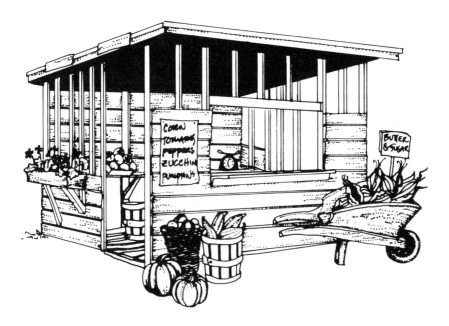

2. **Roadside Stand.** This method is not particularly recommended. If you don't live in a good location you'll have to find and rent one. Your stand itself will cost money to build and paint. You'll need signs, too—not just at the stand but also down the road. You'll have to set it up, be there while it's open, and put everything away—every day. Or you'll have to hire someone to work for you. Not many places can run on a self-service basis, and even a "beep-your-horn" stand requires a lot of your time. (Of course, the kids can help—but will they?) Although you'll make cash sales and get top dollar, you'll also have lots of waste and leftovers. And you'll get no assurance of sales. You'll be at the mercy of traffic and the whim of the public. Talk to any roadside owner— it's a tough way to earn a dollar.

3. **Farmers' Market Stall.** This is similar to a roadside stand, but with a few added drawbacks. You must be there during certain hours, and you'll have the added expense of transportation to and from the market, not to mention rental fees. If it looks attractive, go to one and talk to a few people selling fresh produce.

4. **Door-to-Door.** Remember the pickup truck loaded with fresh produce that used to come around to the neighborhood in the "good ol' days"? Well, it usually wasn't the farmer who drove that truck, but someone who bought the produce at the wholesale market and had a street route. This idea is really a roadside stand or farmers' market stall on wheels. It has all the same advantages and disadvantages of these two approaches, but is more expensive and time-consuming. You might wind up selling more if you establish a dependable route, but it's hard to find many folks at home these days. They're out working or driving the kids somewhere.

Next let's take a look at the wholesale market.

1. **Farmers' or Produce Market.** Not recommended. Here you're in direct competition with the farmers, where you shouldn't even try to compete. Prices are low and your home produce can't compete in the commercial market unless you use lots of fertilizer, insecticides, and water, which will further increase your expenses.

2. **Supermarkets.** Most supermarkets are chain stores owned and operated by some corporation as unrelated to the food industry as you can imagine. Did you know that Grand Union (the eleventh largest supermarket in the country) is a subsidiary of Cavenhorn U.S.A. of Bridgeport, Connecticut, which is a subsidiary of Cavenhorn Ltd. of London, which is controlled by Occidental Holding Company of France, which is partially owned by the French car company, Renault? I'm not suggesting that you have to own a Renault and travel to London or France to get an order, but dealing with a chain might be just as hard in other ways. Most likely the local manager will tell you he's not authorized to buy any new products—he only sells what the main office orders. And where do you go from there?
You might be able to deal with a small, locally owned supermarket, but it will be very demanding on quantity and very low on price. It would be a good-sized order, though, and would keep you busy. Most markets want commercial-type produce because that's what the shoppers expect to see. You'd have to find a market owner willing to feature farm-fresh produce as a supplement to his regular line, and you'd have to practically guarantee a continuous supply, and that's difficult to do from your backyard.

3. **Health Stores.** These have better potential for you if you grow organic produce. "Organically grown" commands a better price and here you'll get it. Of course you'll be paid at wholesale prices. Again, you must produce a large continuous supply of either several specialized crops or many popular crops to keep them happy. They will usually work on a weekly order basis, so you're going to have waste and leftovers. Collecting payment is usually easy if the store is profitable and well-established.

The Best Market

Well, we've looked at the rest—now let's look at the best! In fact, I consider this market to be not only the best, but almost the only one for most situations and locations. It's a place that will welcome you with open arms every time you come; treat you as if you're doing them a favor; buy *everything* you can deliver; and pay you *top retail price, in cash, on the spot.* It's a place that will sign up ahead of time and give you a *continuous market* as long as you can produce, yet will take whatever size harvest you can produce. And it's close to your backyard—usually within five to ten miles. Where's this great Mecca, this goldmine for the square foot gardener? Believe it or not, it's your favorite local restaurant.

When I first started studying possible markets, I didn't even consider the restaurants. I thought surely everyone had already done that, and I wouldn't stand a chance of getting in. But, to my amazement, when I did go to one, the owner said, "Sure, we'd love some fresh homegrown produce." Encouraged, I tried another one, who said, "Bring us all the fresh special lettuce you can grow." Then a gourmet French restaurant owner said, "Can you grow us tender baby carrots, beans, and beets? There's nothing on the market like that." And they were even willing to pay extra for those small, succulent vegetables.

Now I'm not saying every restaurant owner across the country will be gazing out his window waiting for you to arrive. As with any market, there are some good ones and some bad ones, and you may have to do a little selling at first. I've tried them all for several years. Here's some advice that will save you many wasted hours of trudging around from place to place.

First, look for a nice, large, family-style restaurant owned and operated by local people. (Chain restaurants will probably be just like chain supermarkets, so don't bother.) If it's too large, it may be run so efficiently that the owner doesn't want homegrown produce because it's not uniform enough in size and shape. One restaurant couldn't use my tomatoes or cucumbers because they weren't all exactly the same size. This place used slicing machines even for tomatoes, and every one had to look like it came out of a mold. The owner told me, "People don't care what it tastes like, as long as it's uniform and every dish looks the same as their neighbor's." That restaurant is very successful, and you can't argue with success; it just doesn't have good potential for square foot gardeners. The other problem with a place that's too large or efficient is that it is mostly interested in keeping prices down. So you're not going to get top dollar, and your produce isn't going to be appreciated. And who wants to work and not be appreciated?

The next place to stay away from (at least at first) is a very small or specialized restaurant. Its demand for volume will fluctuate so much that you will lose out in the end. Chances are you won't be able to harvest enough of what it needs when it needs it, or else you'll have much more than it can use. Once you're established, you can try the specialized restaurants—French, Italian, steak-and-salad, but wait until the second year for them.

RESTAURANT COMPARISON CHART

	Restaurant 1	Restaurant 2	Restaurant 3
Distance Away			
Seating Capacity			
When Started			
Type Meals			
Clientele			
Know Owner?			
Weekday Volume			
Weekend Volume			
Dinner Only			
Lunch and Dinner			
Days Open			
Like Eating There?			
Want Your Produce Served There?			

How many places should you try to sign up? Only one, or possibly two. Here's the reason: harvesting, delivery, and collection are very time-consuming. If you can take everything to one place, so much the better. You should have a second choice in the back of your mind, just in case something happens to your first choice. (Restaurants do burn down or change hands occasionally.)

How to Find the Best Place

Make a list of all the restaurants within five to ten miles of your garden; then pick the best two or three for final consideration. Compare how far they are from you, how big they are, how long they've been in business, the type of meals served, the type of clientele, whether you or anyone you know is acquainted with the owner, the volume of business done on weekdays as well as on the weekend, whether the restaurant serves lunch as well as dinner, and how many days per week it's open. Last, but not least, is it a place where you would like to eat, and would you be proud of having your produce served there? Write this all down in chart form, and it will be easy to see who comes out on top.

How to Approach Them

Your next step is to see the owner or manager and sell your idea and yourself. Why do you have to sell yourself? Because you're dealing with people, and you first have to convince the owner that he would *like* to deal with you, that you can raise good vegetables, that you will deliver on time and are dependable. All people in business are hesitant to try anything new, not merely because of the uncertainty of being able to sell it (they may be willing to take a chance on that), but because they're unsure of the dependability of the supply or the supplier. If it's wildly successful, what if the new supplier can't deliver fast enough? If it's moderately successful, what if the customers get to depend on it and the supplier gets sick or goes out of business? Many businesses have been "burned" with bad experiences, especially with people who had appealing items or services and tried to supply them from small part-time businesses run from their homes.

Remember that most restaurants have never bought produce from local farms or gardens. They buy from established wholesale restaurant supply firms who purchase in huge quantities and can deliver anything at any time, usually a day or so after the restaurant phones in the order. You, on the other hand, are going to supply an unknown amount of material of untested quality. Getting discouraged? Don't. Remember, your produce will be fresher and will taste incomparably better. So don't be hesitant to sell yourself and your produce.

Sales Plan

I used to use a sales plan that almost sold itself. I'd get all cleaned up in my good garden clothes. If my garden were producing, I'd pack a huge basket of the best-looking, most colorful choice vegetables I could find. I'd wash and shine everything till it sparkled and fill the basket to overflowing. Then I would rush it to the restaurant for a short interview with the owner/manager.

Should you make an appointment? In general, I'd say no. That's contrary to most business advice, but restaurant owners are usually in and available. What I would do is find out the restaurant's slowest time of the day. Then I'd pick a bright, sunny day and phone just before that time to make sure the owner is in and not tied up with his accountant or interviewing a new chef. I wouldn't ask to speak to the owner because he will want to know why you want to see him. It's hard to tell the whole story over the phone, so just take a chance and go in to see him. You may have to wait a little, maybe half an hour, but the only damage will be that your vegetables may wilt a little. Keep them in as cool a place as possible while you're waiting. Don't set them out in the sun or leave the basket in the car.

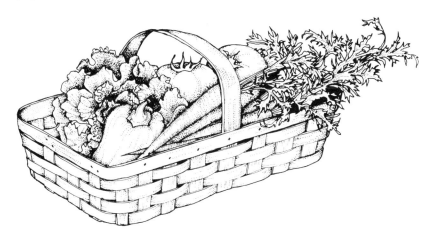

When the owner sees the basket his reaction is usually, "Why, isn't that beautiful!" (If it's not, that's not your restaurant.) Your opening statement should be, "How would you like to get this every day, fresh from my garden to your restaurant?" He'll most likely say yes (or again, this isn't your restaurant). Introduce yourself; tell him where you live and explain a little about square foot gardening. *Tell him you can produce the freshest, best-tasting vegetables—in quantity—and can deliver them within two hours of harvesting. Assure him that every delivery will look like this, with everything selected, culled, and washed.*

After the first flurry of reaction and exchange of information, he will probably say, "But I buy from two big suppliers now and they keep me supplied all year long. You couldn't do that. Besides, I would need twenty crates of lettuce every week—that's 400 heads. How could you do that?"

And here is your biggest, most important selling point (and insurance for staying in business). Tell him that you *don't want, and could never handle, all his business. You would like to deliver enough fresh, choice salad fixings each week to amount to about 20 percent of his total needs. Your produce would only supplement his present supplies.*

QUOTES FROM RESTAURANTS AROUND THE COUNTRY

- "I'd like to drive out to the farm stands—but we never seem to have the time—so I'll take whatever you can bring me."

- "Where did you ever get such good looking lettuce, and can I buy some? I'll take all you can deliver every week."

- "I really like the idea that it's local grown and farm fresh."

- "Now we can get things riper with more flavor."

- "I'm *always* looking for fresh produce."

- "This would save me a three-hour round trip every week! If all your lettuce looks like this, I'll give you $1 a head and take any amount you can bring me every week."

- "This is the best looking produce I've ever seen. We have to throw out 20 percent of what we normally get from our regular supply house. There would be no waste with yours, so I could pay you more."

- "Our summer volume is up so I could use more produce."

This approach has several advantages to both you and your prospective employer. First, the volume you produce six months of the year won't seriously affect the business of the larger suppliers. They won't even consider you much of a competitor. You'll be like a small, pesky fly to them. (Larger, very pesky flies are more likely to get swatted.) Since you're supplying only 20 percent of the restaurant's needs, it won't become dependent on you and panic if you show up with only 10 percent one day. Conversely, it will also be able to handle easily all you can produce if you show up with 30 percent on some days.

See the advantage to you? You sell everything you can produce, and you don't have to fool around with orders.

You must convince the owner that it's to both your advantages if you deliver whatever is ready and at its peak. He'll get better produce and you'll sell everything you can raise. Every restaurant owner I visited went along with this proposal. In fact, you should suggest that he try a little of everything until you get to know what he prefers and the quantities he requires.

Learn His Likes

Even gardeners tend to forget how much time must elapse between planting the seeds and harvesting the produce. You'll have a lot of planning and scheduling to do, so the next step is to get some idea of the different vegetables he would like, and in what quantities. You should know what you can grow well in your area, as well as what will give you a profitable harvest, before you discuss this with the owner. Ask him how many cases of lettuce he uses in an average week; how many bunches of carrots or beets; how many pounds of string beans, tomatoes, cucumbers, etc. (Don't forget to ask how many heads are in a case or carrots in a bunch.)

Then discuss varieties. You should bring along a seed catalog so you can show him pictures of the different varieties of leaf lettuce, the shapes and sizes of carrots, etc. As you well know, a colorful seed catalog is a powerful selling tool all by itself. (Remember how many varieties you're tempted to order every winter?) You can bring a list of those vegetables you're prepared to raise or just mark them in your seed catalog.

Talking Money

Now for the tough part of your sales presentation: the price. Don't be shy about talking dollars. Now's the time. You have the owner interested and probably all excited about this new idea. At this very moment, he's dreaming about having the only restaurant in town that will serve fresh, home grown produce. Review what you're going to deliver: the *freshest* (within one or two hours of harvest), choicest, *locally grown* (stress that point—it's a pride point), best-tasting vegetables around. If you're growing organically and he's interested in that, mention it again. *Then* tell him your price. Say, "I'm willing to grow especially for you. I'll deliver the produce whenever you want it, all washed and sorted, for the same price as you would pay at the nearest farm stand."

Don't mention wholesale prices or restaurant suppliers. No comparison should be drawn; in fact, commercially grown produce shouldn't even be considered in the same breath with yours. The only thing that could possibly come close would be local farm produce. So you can compare farm stand prices with yours, except that *you* deliver free, produce a better crop, and will plant especially for his needs. Keep referring to your basket sitting there. If your beans or carrots haven't wilted from all this heavy talk, nibble a few every once in a while. Offer him a crisp carrot or a sweet-tasting leaf of lettuce.

Explain how you will deliver on any day and time that's *mutually convenient,* that you'll include an itemized bill at the current prices, and that you'll unload and help put away the produce before collecting. (That's a polite and subtle way to say you'd like to be paid at the time of delivery.)

If you get the reply, "We pay all bills by check," or "We pay once a month," explain that to keep down the cost to him, you would like to run this business (don't call it a hobby) in as simple a manner as possible, and ask, "You can understand that, can't you?" Explain that you'd like to devote all of your time and talents to raising the best possible vegetables rather than to a lot of bookkeeping and banking, and you'd appreciate it very much if he could go along with this, especially since, compared to his volume of business, you're just a little guy, and just starting out. (He'll remember the day he started, and he'll probably wish he could return to those days when it was so simple to run a business.)

Now you're down to the final point: will he or won't he? Many potential sales are lost because the salesman is afraid to ask, "Will you buy?" All the books and articles on salesmanship stress this important step called "closing the sale." Why is the salesman afraid to ask? Well, it's because of a very basic trait of human nature: we're afraid of failure. So, if you don't ask, they can't say "no." The natural tendency for many people is to thank the person for his time and interest, leave an order form, and get out of there with everyone smiling. You hope he will fill out the order form later. That's the easy way, but unfortunately it's not good business.

QUESTIONS TO ASK THE RESTAURANT OWNER

Ask the owner or chef
during the first interview:

Would you like some farm fresh locally grown produce?

What volume do you use each week?

swiss chard	radishes	cucumbers
spinach	scallions	tomatoes
leaf lettuce	peppers	cherry tomatoes
cos lettuce	eggplant	beans

Do you use any unusual vegetables?

bok choy	Japanese turnips
Chinese cabbage	sugar snap peas

Is there anything special I could grow for you?

What is the best day and time for delivery?

Would you like my fresh harvest for the weekend trade?

Would you be willing to help me get started?

An easy way to ask the final question is to make the answer easy. For example, "How many bunches of parsley will you need every week?" "What's the best delivery day for you?" Or simply, "Would you be willing to try this idea to help me get started?"

If the owner seems reluctant, find out why and then see if you can't reason him out of his objections. If he says, "We don't know how well special lettuce will be accepted," then answer, "Let's try just a little at first and keep most of it to the more common varieties." His question: "What if your crop is a failure, or you get sick and can't supply us?" Your answer: "I'm planting quite a variety of different crops at different times, so if one particular crop fails it won't have much effect. If I get sick, my wife (son-in-law, whoever) will be helping me and can take over. And since we're only supplying 20 percent of your fresh vegetable needs, no great catastrophe can occur."

A display of your vegetables often will convince the restaurant chef.

If he still wants to think about it, your chances don't look too good. Don't be discouraged, but go on to your second choice right away. Even if the first restaurant says, "We'll try it and see," I'd go on to the second one and sign it up so you have two. Only when the first restaurant is very enthusiastic would I rely on one place for all my business. You might go to the second or third and at least talk to it about your ideas; get reactions and say, "When I'm ready to harvest, could I come back to talk to you again?" If that restaurant is at all interested, you'll get a "yes," but you haven't committed yourself in case something else comes along.

If you close the sale, write the plan out on paper so he fully understands it and can keep a record in his files. So many misunderstandings are over "I didn't think you meant that," or "I thought you said you were going to do this." Since you both said a lot during your first meeting, put the agreement in writing and leave room at the bottom for two signatures. Have it typed, keeping it *as simple and short as possible.* Don't try to be a lawyer, and for heaven's sake don't go out and get one. He'll only complicate the deal and expand a simple one-page agreement into four pages to justify his fee. Your agreement should merely state what you're going to provide and what the restaurant will do.

Dear Restaurant Owner:

This letter may serve as our agreement for the purchase of fresh vegetables.

1. _____ agrees to grow and harvest choice select vege-
       Gardener's name
   tables for sale to _____ for the
                           Restaurant name
   growing season of 19_____ .

2. All vegetables will be sorted, culled, washed, and cleaned of waste material, and delivered within a few hours of harvesting.

3. An itemized list showing quantities and current farm stand prices will accompany each delivery. Cash payment will be made upon completion of delivery.

4. Delivery will be made twice a week on _____ and _____ at approximately _____ o'clock a.m./p.m.

5. _____ will try to grow those varieties particularly
       Gardener's name
   requested, and each delivery shall consist of whatever is currently ready for harvest without regard to exact quantities.

6. All food shall be grown by strictly organic methods, using no chemical fertilizer, no chemical insecticides. (Include only if it applies.)

7. _____ agrees to act as an independent contractor/
       Gardener's name
   supplier and neither party will hold the other liable for any of his operation or business.

_____   _____
        Gardener's signature   Date

_____   _____
    Restaurant owner's signature   Date

The restaurant owner might ask you to add to that agreement this paragraph:

8. Either party can terminate the agreement with ten days' written notice if produce, prices, or conditions are unsatisfactory.

A lawyer would add all kinds of things like, "This agreement is binding to both parties and will be assumed by any new owner, heirs, etc.," but it all boils down to two parties' desire to get together. If one wants out, no written agreement is going to keep him in. You'd have to hire a lawyer to enforce any agreement, and who needs that?

Why have an agreement at all, you might ask. Only to make sure that both parties know the general conditions of the agreement and are sincere enough to sign their names to it.

What if the owner won't sign, but is willing to go ahead on a verbal say-so? Well, you'll have to decide whether he is trustworthy, honest, and sincere in wanting to try this plan. Many people won't sign their names to anything because the very idea makes them suspicious. Don't try to change people's personalities. Just accept them and proceed with enthusiasm and hope.

The Timing

Do you start planting and then go out to sign up restaurants, or do you try to get your customers first? It all depends on the season in which you read this book and decide to start your own cash garden. If it's winter, I'd plan the garden, order the seeds, search the restaurants for the best three, and in early spring go see one (without a basket of vegetables). In the meantime, I'd plant a full crop because I'd be sure to find at least one good customer.

If I read the book in the spring, I'd do all of the above, but very quickly! If it's summer when I decide, I'd pick a harvest basket from my present garden and sign up a place or two for the fall and next spring. If it's fall, unless you plant ahead, you're not going to have enough in your present garden to make it worthwhile for you to deliver to the owner. In fact, you may kill the whole deal if he decides it's too much bother for such a small amount and says no for next year. So it's better to take a basket in and sign him up for next year.

YOU'VE DECIDED TO TRY IT

If you decide in....	You can plant and harvest all....
Winter	Spring, summer, fall
Spring	Summer, fall
Summer	Fall
Fall	Wait until next year, but be ready.

Note: If you live along the southern or western coast, you can add a winter crop to all of the above seasons.

Health Food Stores

If you garden organically, there is one market that runs a poor second to restaurants, and that is health food stores or very small, specialized grocery stores. I would look into these if I couldn't find a restaurant that would buy from me. They would probably order enough to make it worthwhile, and might be willing to mix your produce with their regular supply. Again, don't try to meet all their needs, or you will be in trouble. Let them order, then grow more of everything to insure that you can fill that order. To do this every week, all season long, takes a lot of planning, skill, and good luck.

What about prices at the health food stores? They pay wholesale prices, but they only want organically grown, so that automatically commands a 30 to 40 percent premium over standard prices. For example, if farm stand bibb lettuce is 69¢ per head, that same lettuce, organically grown, is 40 percent higher or 99¢ per head retail. Wholesale is 50 percent of retail, so you would get 50 percent times 99¢ or 49¢ per head for organic lettuce at the health food store. That's a lot below the restaurant giving you 69¢ per head. In fact, if you figure that it costs you about 29¢ per head for your time, material, land use, equipment, and non-saleable harvest, then your profit amounts to 40¢ from the restaurant, but only 20¢ for the store. This is why it's so important to get retail prices rather than settle for wholesale.

Organic or health food restaurants are another great possibility, but again they are usually small and limited in the number of meals they serve. However, they will usually pay top dollar. Now we're looking at farm stand plus organic premium prices of 99¢ with a resulting profit of 70¢. Since they're small in comparison with regular restaurants, they will probably want to place orders and have you fill all their needs if possible. Some special arrangements can always be made—just ask.

I had one who paid top dollar and took everything I had to supplement his regular supply, but this turned out to be a disaster. One day when I arrived with a particularly nice, large harvest, he said, without any warning or advance notice, "I can't use that. Business is bad, and I don't need anything." He almost ruined my business! I had a whole truckload of fresh lettuce and it was a boiling hot summer's day. If the lettuce wasn't refrigerated within an hour I'd be out $75 of hard-earned money. Not only that, think of all the produce in the garden that I had planted for him that would be ready during the next few weeks.

I quickly went to one organic food store who didn't handle fresh produce but was willing to try some, and an organic co-op grocery who took the rest to try it. Neither of those places worked out; they were too small and wanted to order a case of this and a case of that once a week. You can't make a profit that way, selling whatever you can from your garden at whatever price you can get. Luckily, my main restaurant customer could absorb all of our harvest, and for the rest of the year I settled into an easy one-customer routine. What if I lost that one? I had talked to another large restaurant who said it might be interested, so I had one in reserve.

Pitfalls, Too

So you can see there are pitfalls in this business, too. But the rewards are so far above any other part-time business I've ever tried or even read about. You're outdoors, in your own backyard, doing something you love, and earning several thousand dollars a year in extra income. You can't ask for much more than that. To be really successful, you must be willing to spend a little extra time investigating the best restaurant prospects and selling them on your new business idea.

One last point, for those of you that think there are no good restaurants nearby. I've had some people say, "Oh, sure, you live in a prosperous suburban area with lots of fancy restaurants, but we live out in the sticks with few, if any, good restaurants." Let me tell you I've been out in the sticks, too, and if you open your eyes and look around you can find a good customer.

We were in a very small town in South Carolina filming our TV show and stayed at the local Holiday Inn. For dinner, I picked the special of the day, the Chef's Boston Bibb Salad. But the waitress said, "We're all out of the bibb lettuce." The next day we were filming at one of the seed companies' test gardens and were doing harvest scenes. I filled a huge plastic bag with all kinds of lettuce, including Boston bibb and Chinese cabbage, and took it into the kitchen that night, dumped the lettuce on the counter in front of the head chef, and said, "Now will you make me a Chef's Special Boston Bibb Salad?"

He said, "Where did you get your beautiful lettuce and can I buy some from you?"

Well, the upshot was that I did an interview with him the next day, and he told me that most Holiday Inns around the country were independently owned and the head chef had the authority to buy produce from whomever he wanted.

This chef was willing to pay a premium, even more than farm stand prices for my lettuce, and was talking about advertising in the local papers about his special home-grown produce. Of course, I had to tell him I didn't live in the area. But he and many other chefs are still there waiting for you to come in. Incidentally, I gave him the lettuce, and he made me the most wonderful salad I've ever had.

I got thinking of how many new buyers this experience could mean. There must be a Holiday Inn in every small town in the country (as well as several in every metropolitan area) and where there isn't one, there must be a Ramada, or Quality Court or some motel with a restaurant. The number of outlets is unlimited around the country, so find one that fits your needs.

Chapter 5

What to Grow

 Now that you've decided to start your part-time square foot gardening venture and have lined up one or two potential customers, the next step is to decide what to grow.

Your decision will probably be influenced by what you like to grow. But there are other questions.

1. What grows well in your part of the country?

2. What grows well in your yard?

3. Which crops do your buyers want?

4. What will sell for the most money?

5. Which crops are easiest to grow?

After a little thinking and research, you will be able to answer these questions. Here are a few tips from my own experience that may help.

Vegetables such as lettuce, radishes, and spinach not only sell well, as do tomatoes, cucumbers, and peppers, but they are fairly easy to grow in just about any state.

Others, such as cabbages, onions, and potatoes, take a long time to grow; moreover, many buyers think there's not much difference between your crops and those from a commercial grower—an onion is an onion. We know it's not true, but you might have a difficult time convincing your customers to buy "special" homegrown onions.

As would be expected, the more durable, easily shipped, and easily stored a vegetable is, the more difficult it will be for you to compete with commercial growers who raise it.

The lesson from all this: raise the more fragile and delicate tasting crops. For example, no one will dispute that your vine-ripened red beauties taste far better than commercial tomatoes, the kind that can roll down Route 66 through three states without a bruise.

WHAT TO RAISE

The most productive and profitable crops

Leaf lettuce	Swiss chard
Cherry tomatoes	Radishes
Cucumbers	

CROPS THAT DO BEST IN COOL SEASONS

Asparagus	Chicory	Kale	Potato
Beet	Chin. Cabbage	Kohlrabi	Radish
Broad bean	Chives	Leek	Rhubarb
Broccoli	Collards	Lettuce	Rutabaga
Br. sprouts	Corn salad	Mustard	Salsify
Cabbage	Cress	Onion	Swiss chard
Carrot	Endive	Pak choi	Shallot
Cauliflower	Florence fennel	Parsley	Sorrel
Celery	Garlic	Parsnip	Spinach
Celeriac	Horse radish	Pea	Turnip
			Watercress

CROPS THAT DO BEST IN WARM SEASONS

Beans	Lima beans	Soybean
Corn	Muskmelon	Summer squash
Cowpea	New Zealand	Sweet potato
(Southern pea)	spinach	Tomato
Cucumber	Okra	Watermelon
Eggplant	Pumpkin	Winter squash

MINIMUM SUNLIGHT REQUIREMENTS

Partial Sun (4-6 hours a day)	Full Sun (over 6 hours a day)
Crops with edible leaves or roots	*Crops with fruit type harvest*
Beets	Beans
Carrots	Corn
Cauliflower	Eggplant
Swiss chard	Muskmelons
Lettuce	Summer squash
Onions	Tomatoes
Parsley	
Peas	
Radishes	
Spinach	

What's Most Profitable?

Most everyone wants to know what crop produces the most dollars per square foot. But that isn't the only consideration. You must also consider how long that crop takes to grow. So you should ask, "What crop produces the most dollars per square foot per season or growing period?"

For example, one tomato plant, when grown by the vertical method, takes up only one square foot for the entire growing season. It also produces more fruit than a plant grown by the traditional sprawl method that takes up nine square feet.

How Much Work?

Another consideration is the amount of work required during a plant's growth. Radishes grow quickly, but there is constant labor in planting the seeds, thinning, weeding, watering, and, finally, harvesting. Even the labor involved in harvesting can vary from crop to crop. Tomatoes are picked off the vine and put in a box to be weighed, while radishes, carrots, and lettuce must be pulled or cut, washed, counted, and packed.

Prices Will Vary

You should also remember that prices vary, from month to month and around the country. The prices in the chart are used only to draw a comparison between our examples. Don't use them as quotes to your buyer. I will help you figure out exactly what you should charge for your produce. Basically, we want to analyze how much there is to harvest, how much that harvest will bring on the open market, and how long it takes to grow that harvest, including any extra work or problems we can anticipate.

But we'll boil everything down to one chart that gives us a reasonable comparison: how many dollars you can earn per crop, per square foot, per unit of time (in this case, one month). Obviously, you'll be gardening for more than one month, and a lot of plants will take a lot longer than one month to reach maturity.

SELECTING YOUR CROPS

Pick your crops so they fit into the time you have available for gardening.

If you teach school, you won't have as much time for gardening in the spring and fall as you will in the summer. The opposite will be true if you have a summer job in the recreational field.

Quick crops like radishes and lettuce are not only profitable but won't tie you down to a long-term commitment. On the other hand, they do require a lot of weekly activity, planting and harvesting them.

Long-term vegetables like tomatoes, peppers, and eggplant take very little weekly maintenance but produce no income until they are harvested. Then they yield continuously, with very little work on your part.

Probably the best solution is a combination of the two types. That should keep you busy and making a profit all of the time, and never overworked or underpaid.

In order to help you decide, study the accompanying table of the most popular vegetables to grow. Combine this information with local prices, estimate the profitability of various crops, then set up your plans for a cash garden.

TYPICAL YIELD FROM A CASH SQUARE FOOT GARDEN

Vegetable	Unit of Measure	Harvest Per Sq. Foot	Average Price/$	Total Sale	Months to Grow	Index No. $/Month /Sq. Foot
Lettuce	Head	4	.79	3.16	2	1.60
Cherry Tomatoes	Pound	6	1.39	8.34	6	1.40
Cucumbers	Each	30	.19	5.70	6	.95
Swiss Chard	Bunch	21	.29	6.09	7	.85
Radishes	Each	16	.05	.80	1	.80
Snap Beans	Pound	2	.79	1.58	2	.80
Tomatoes	Pound	9	.49	4.41	6	.75
Carrots	Each	16	.12	1.92	3	.65
Peppers	Pound	8	.39	3.12	6	.50
Eggplant	Pound	4	.49	1.96	6	.35
Corn	Ear	2	.20	.40	3	.15

If we leave out corn and eggplant, the average is 90¢ per month per square foot for a six-month season. That's equal to $5.40 per square foot. That means a garden that measures 640 square feet, like the one on the cover of this book, could take in an average of 640 x $5.40 = $3,500 per year. By selecting the more profitable crops, that could be almost doubled, to $6,000 per year.

But by multiplying the number of months of your local harvest season by these figures, you'll arrive at an approximate idea of the income you might realize.

These figures are also based on square feet of actual growing space, rather than your total garden area. Do not count the areas necessary for aisles and paths (the non-productive areas). But you'll still be pleasantly surprised to discover how much you can earn from your backyard garden.

How You Decide

How you go about deciding what to grow will depend just as much on your personality as on facts and figures. One person might feed a large amount of data into a personal computer, including such factors as quality, pest resistance, and weather resistance. He would then come up with an elaborate system for predicting the crops that will produce the largest harvest for the maximum dollars in the shortest amount of time and the smallest space, and at the least risk of failure from pests and weather. Another person might wake up one morning and say, "I'm going to grow lettuce, string beans, radishes, and a few tomatoes, and that's it." One person might decide to specialize in just one crop and become the spinach king of the lower valley, or the lettuce queen of the entire county. Another might grow nothing but twelve varieties of tomatoes. Each has his own reasons and thinks his crop is best suited to his conditions—and it probably is.

But will a restaurant owner buy nothing but tomatoes from you, or lettuce, or even radishes? The answer is "yes." He will accept almost anything you can offer if it's better than the next person's produce.

How Difficult?

Other considerations will be the difficulty of growing each crop, the amount of time required to harvest it and prepare it for delivery, and the feasibility of storing it.

For example, tomatoes are quick and easy to harvest, and they can just sit there for hours and not deteriorate. Lettuce doesn't hold up that well, especially if left outside in the sun for any length of time. In addition it has to be washed, and that means constantly changing the wash water, another time-consuming chore. Yet we can see that, in price, lettuce outperforms tomatoes two to one. You just have to decide if it's worth the extra work and whether you can find the time in your daily schedule.

Another consideration: how risky is the crop? Could disease wipe you out overnight, with, as in the case of tomatoes, no time to grow another crop? You'd be wiped out for the season, whereas a quick crop such as radishes could be destroyed by pests, weather, or disease, and you could be back in business with a new crop in just four weeks.

None of these considerations is earth-shattering in itself, and I don't want to give you the impression that they are too complicated for you to handle. They're just normal, everyday possibilities that every business person has to consider.

We all confront, and handle, endless "what-ifs" in the course of our lives. The decisions you make in running a small business won't require any more know-how or common sense than you've already got.

Let's look at an example. Suppose you decide to go after the fragile crops because they usually bring a much higher price. You must consider that their risk of failure is higher too. What if the weather is bad for a long stretch and your tomatoes don't ripen properly, or a whole flat of raspberries gets crushed in transit? Then there is the matter of storage. Even though most, if not all, of your delivery will be placed in a cooler at the restaurant, will it remain fresh and tasty if the buyer doesn't use it within a few days? Will he

TYPICAL YIELDS
For a 4X4 Square Foot Growing Area

Item	Plants per Square foot	Yield Per 4X4	Avg. Price	Total Sale	Time to Produce
Leaf Lettuce	4	64 heads	.79	$50.50	2 months
Radishes	16	256	.05	12.80	1 month
Beans	9	32 pounds	.79	25.30	2 months
Carrots	16	256	.12	30.72	3 months
Peppers	1	128 pounds	.39	49.90	6 months

You can see that if your buyer can take 50 to 60 radishes per week, you would have to plant four square feet every week for a continuous harvest. (16 x 4 = 64)

be unhappy and then unwilling to buy more? At first glance, that doesn't seem to be your responsibility, but unfortunately it will affect your business. That's why I'll go into detail in chapter seven about taking extraordinary steps to protect your harvest after it's delivered. It's not only added insurance, but it's good business as well.

HOW MUCH SPACE?

If your space is limited, this will obviously influence what you grow. Although we are going to boil all the information down to dollars per square foot, you may want to grow more of the compact space-saving crops such as radishes, scallions, carrots, and lettuce rather than bushier space-taking crops like peppers, eggplant, broccoli, and cabbage.

For example, if you wanted to specialize in leaf and cos lettuce and found a restaurant that would take 40 heads of each per week, your income would be 40 heads x 2 types x .79 = $63.20 per week or $1,640 for a six-month growing season.

The space you would need would be 80 heads per week ÷ 4 heads per square foot = 20 square feet times 8 weeks to grow a crop = 160 sq. ft. That's the size of two 4x20 beds, a very small garden indeed. If you wanted to earn over $3,000 a year you would need four of those beds. Allowing a one-foot path between beds, that's a total yard area of only 20 x 20 feet. Of course, these are all rounded numbers and do not take into account several variables. You'll need extra plants (about 10 percent) for those that don't grow well, but on the other hand you could use transplants started from seed and you wouldn't need the garden space for the full eight weeks, perhaps only six weeks. The end result will be a lot of money in your pocket from a very small space, and with very little work.

Other Considerations

These are the most important considerations. There are a few minor ones, such as the size of the harvest and the size of your car or van. You'll soon realize that $25 worth of lettuce takes up a lot more room than $25 worth of radishes and tomatoes. Also, the lettuce is dripping wet when you're ready to load it into your truck, a situation you may find less than appealing.

In planning your garden, keep in mind that what you think would be best to grow and sell may not turn out to be the best when you get into business. Weather and buyer conditions will also change your plans somewhat. Don't be too rigid in your plans. And, for heaven's sake, don't think that everything has to be perfectly planned before you start. You don't have to have every detail worked out in

Profits from Lettuce

By planting 10 square feet each week of both cos and leaf lettuce, each bed would hold an eight-week supply of lettuce and provide a $63 a week income. This 10x20 area would take approximately four hours a week to plant, tend, harvest, and deliver, and would yield a total seasonal income of $1,640. A 20x20 area would yield over $3,000 a year for seven or eight hours a week labor.

Leaf Lettuce
80 sq. ft. of growing soil

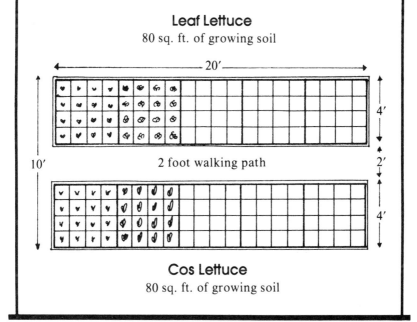

2 foot walking path

Cos Lettuce
80 sq. ft. of growing soil

advance, and what's more, you can't. So don't go to a lot of work and expense developing an elaborate system, only to find that it needs major adjustments. Think your plan through, write down a summary, talk it over with friends and family, get your buyer all excited and ready to go, and then get started. Believe me, you can do it.

FILL IN YOUR GARDEN SPACE NEEDED

Crop	Number of Plants	Plants Per Square Ft.	Square Feet Required	Number of Plantings	Total Garden Space Needed
Continuous Harvest; *Plant Once, Seeds and Transplants*					
Cucumbers		2		1	
Eggplant		1		1	
Peppers		1		1	
Squash		1		1	
Tomatoes		1		1	
Limited Harvest; *Replant Every Two Weeks, Seeds*					
Pole beans		8		2	
Bush beans		9		6	
Peas		8		2	
Single Harvest; *Replant Weekly, Transplants*					
Broccoli		1		1	
Cabbage		1		1	
Cauliflower		1		1	
Lettuce		4		4	
Spinach		9		4	
Single Harvest; *Replant Weekly, Seeds*					
Beets		9		8	
Radishes		16		4	
Turnips		9		6	
Scallions		25		6	

A Typical Cash Garden

For your initial crop selection, it's best to grow a little of everything. That way, you can see how it goes, both in the growing and selling.

Try to stick to the common and easily grown varieties. Divide your garden area into long- and short-season crops.

Of course, you are going to have vertical as well as low-growing varieties. For the vertical ones, grow tomatoes and cucumbers. Leave melons and squash until later on. Get a mixture of early-, mid-, and late-season tomatoes. That will stretch out your harvest and give you small, medium, and large tomatoes to sell. Don't forget cherry tomatoes. They sell well, and most restaurants use a lot of them. Make sure you select disease-resistant plants. You don't want to fool around with something like a wilt disease, which could wipe you out in mid-season.

For cucumbers, try some of the standard varieties as well as the burpless. Put in a few Chinese—those long, skinny ones. If your buyer is not familiar with them, point out that they're sweet, mild, free of seeds, easy to prepare, and the ideal size to serve sliced on a salad plate without having to cut them in half.

Hank Ellis proudly picks prizewinning tomatoes in his cash garden.

Try several varieties of peppers. Grow only a few hot pepper plants. If your buyer doesn't want them, you might find a pizza parlor that would love fresh, homegrown, hot peppers. In fact, they might want to take all the peppers that you have. Don't go too heavily into the yellow or the banana types, or any other unusual shapes. Most buyers want standard green bell peppers.

The same goes for eggplant. It might be very hard to sell the white, yellow, or brown varieties. You'll even find resistance to the long, skinny Chinese or ichiban varieties, but you might discover an Oriental restaurant that would love them.

Bush and Pole Beans

Bush or pole beans are good producers and store well after picking, but take time to harvest. A gourmet restaurant might like the tiny, half-size French beans. Such restaurants will pay extra for this size, but keep in mind that it takes a lot more of them to equal the same weight or volume of full-size beans.

Consider peas in the spring and fall. They are big producers, take up very little space when grown vertically, and are fast growers. I would suggest that you stay with the sugar snap varieties, either the original six-foot Sugar Snap peas or the shorter bush varieties such as Sugar Ann, Sugar Mel, or Sugar Ray.

Lettuce Crops

You'll want at least three or four varieties of leaf lettuce. Don't bother with head lettuce. It takes a long time to grow and needs a lot of water and special care. Besides, it is very fickle about the weather. Stay with leaf or bibb lettuce. There are many varieties that are quick and easy to grow, and they always bring a good price. Try a mixture of bibb or butterhead, and leaf.

Although the red varieties of leaf lettuce are my favorite, I have found restaurant buyers are not as excited over the unusual or exotic. Stick with the green standard varieties like the Black-Seeded Simpson and Salad Bowl. The cos or romaine lettuce is also popular and sells very well. It has an upright head, is very easy to grow, and produces a lot of leaves. The other leaf crops such as Swiss chard, beet leaves, kale, and collards are not as much in demand, so even though they are easy to grow, I wouldn't put in too many plants. The most popular leaf crop is probably spinach, but it does well only in cool weather. Lettuce can be grown with shade and lots of water in the hot weather; spinach cannot.

Root Crops

Root crops sell well, are easy to grow through the entire season, and are always in demand. Carrots, beets, radishes, and scallions are the main ones. There is a vast difference in growing time between carrots and radishes. Radishes, being a quick crop, require a lot more planting, harvesting, and replanting. The labor involved is repeated almost three times while you are growing just one crop of carrots, and those carrots require virtually no work. They just sit there and grow, night and day. All you need is good, loose, friable soil and lots of water while they're growing.

Growing Scallions

Scallions are different. They can be started with either seeds or sets. Seeds are cheaper, but sets produce a quicker crop. Realizing that it is the white, tender part, grown below the soil surface, that everyone eats, I got to thinking, "Why not plant the sets or seeds deeper than normal?" Then everything below ground would be white and you wouldn't have to hill up the scallions to get that white portion covered. Less work.

After a few experiments, I came up with the perfect way to grow scallions, and a lot in one square foot. In addition, these scallions will have twice the amount of white, tender stalk as a regular scallion.

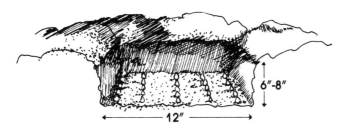

For the best scallions, dig a hole this size, plant and cover 25 onion sets, and gradually add more soil as sprouts grow.

For a small backyard garden, we dig out one square foot, straight down about six or eight inches, removing all the soil. (Your natural soil must be well drained to do this.) You thus create a square foot hole. Your soil won't cave in if it's fairly moist, and it should be in a square foot garden. Loosen the subsoil. Add a little organic matter and fertilizer to the bottom soil. Make sure you test and adjust your pH to between 6 and 7.

Space out room for twenty-five sets. Do this by drawing two lines, making four squares in the square foot. Poke a hole in the exact center of the square foot, then, with two fingers at a time, poke twin holes four times along the lines, then two twin holes in each of the small squares. You now have twenty-five holes, and you can plant the sets.

Push them in until their tips are just at the surface. Cover with about an inch of good soil mix, then water with a fine sprinkler can. In about a week you will have twenty-five green sprouts. Remember, your soil level is still four to six inches below the surrounding area.

Now here's the best part of this new concept. Each week add just enough screened compost or special square foot garden soil mix to cover those sprouts. They will keep growing very rapidly, pushing up through the soil as you add it, and in a few weeks, by adding soil you will bring the surface up to the surrounding garden.

You can start pulling the scallions any time you need them. They will keep growing, becoming fatter and taller. If you leave them too long they will develop bulbs on the bottom, trying to make a large, regular onion, but you will pull them long before that.

Just think—you'll harvest twenty-five double-size scallions in just six weeks, from only one square foot. Restaurants use a lot of scallions, so plan on quite a few square feet for them. Of course, for a cash garden, you'll dig out and plant several square feet at a time.

Can you charge twice the going price since yours are twice the size of the usual scallions? Talk this over with your buyer, but probably he will want to pay the same price. To a diner a scallion is a scallion, no matter what its size.

Little Profit in Corn

How about corn? It takes up a lot of room, takes a long time to grow, and has a lot of pests. Besides, it yields the lowest profit for any vegetable.

When I learned that farmers growing corn earn only $200 to $300 per acre, or about half a cent per square foot, I started thinking how a farmer could earn more from his land. This led to a study of the smaller truck farm operations, which in turn led me to think about cash returns from a backyard garden. It is one thing to improve the productivity of a garden five-fold with the square foot system, but there had to be a new and different market for that harvest. Well, you know the rest of the story from chapter four. It can be done, and you, no matter where you live, can earn hundreds, if not thousands of dollars, from your hobby using this simple and practical system.

Don't try to imitate the farmers in selecting your crops. Remember square foot is not only a totally different way to garden, it is a totally new way to market your produce, and you must always keep your market in mind when making your selections.

PLANT SEEDS DIRECTLY IN GARDEN

Vegetable	Spacing Per Sq. Foot	Hardy or Non-Hardy	Safe to Plant Outdoors ____ Weeks Before Last Frost
Beans (bush)	9	NH	0
Beans (pole)	8	NH	0
Beets	9	H	3
Carrots	16	H	3
Cucumbers	2	NH	1 week after
Peas		H	5
Radishes	16	H	3
Squash (Summer)	1	NH	0
Squash (Winter)	1	NH	2 weeks after

PLANT TRANSPLANTS IN GARDEN

Vegetable	Spacing Per Sq. Foot	Hardy or Non-Hardy	Safe to Plant Outdoors ____ Weeks Before Last Frost
Broccoli	1	H	5
Cabbage	1	H	5
Cauliflower	1	H	4
Eggplant	1	NH	2 weeks after
Leaf Lettuce	4	H	4
Peppers	1	NH	2 weeks after
Scallions	25	H	4
Spinach	9	H	4
Squash (Summer)		NH	0
Squash (Winter)	1	NH	2 weeks after
Swiss Chard	4	NH	3
Tomatoes	1	NH	0

Time from Seeds to Harvest	Season to Grow				Fertilize Every ___ Weeks	Replant Every ___ Weeks
	S	Sm	F	SF		
8		•		•	2	2
9		•		•	2	—
8	•	•	•		2	2
10	•	•	•		2	2
9		•		•	2	—
10	•		•		2	—
4	•	•	•		No extra	1
8		•		•	2	—
12		•		•	2	—

Note: S = Spring Sm = Summer F = Fall
SF = Add Spring and Fall for Southern U.S.

Weeks From Seeds to Transplants	Weeks From Transplants to Harvest	Season to Grow				Fertilize Every ___ Weeks	Replant Every ___ Weeks
		S	Sm	F	SF		
7	9	•		•		2	2
7	9	•		•		2	2
6	8	•		•		2	2
9	10		•		•	2	—
3	4	•	•	•		1	1
9	10		•		•	2	—
6	8	•	•	•		1	1
3	4	•		•		1	1
2	6		•		•	1	—
2	12		•			2	—
4	4	•	•	•		1	—
6	11		•		•	2	—

Chapter 6

How Much
to Charge

$ This chapter may do more to ensure your success than any
other in the book. Proper pricing—how much you
charge—can mean the difference between success and failure, just paying for your seeds and supplies and making enough for
a vacation or to pay off some big bills.

We'll explore not only how to set prices for your produce, but
how to convince your customer that your produce is worth the top
figure that you're asking.

You will probably be surprised to learn that the prices you can
charge may vary by as much as 100 percent. That's because we're
talking about the difference between wholesale and retail prices.
One is about twice as much as the other.

Breakdown of Prices

These are the prices at the end of a whole chain of gradual
increases along the way. For example, the farmer who grows the
wheat for a $1 package of dinner rolls receives about a nickel for his
plowing, planting, growing, and harvesting. Part of that nickel, too,
must cover the cost of his land and equipment, and his employees'
salaries. The person who transports, stores, and sells the wheat gets
a dime. And along almost every step of the way the price doubles to
pay various middlemen. By the time that wheat is processed into
flour, sold to a bakery, baked, packaged, and delivered to your
supermarket, the cost has gone up to fifty cents. When you, the
consumer, pay $1 for the rolls, you've provided jobs for a complete
chain of free enterprise, and you've paid some local and federal
taxes. Although it may seem that some along the way are getting

more than they deserve, no one is making a huge profit. You might think that $1 is too much for the store to charge. But when you deduct overhead, salaries, spoilage, and leftovers, the store ends up making less than 10 percent profit, which is about average for most businesses. In fact, everyone along the line probably makes about the same profit percentage.

In the fresh produce business, the grower or farmer gets a higher percentage. This is because the basic commodity is not converted into another product, as is done with wheat.

Here is a typical breakdown of each dollar of the greengrocer's business: the grower gets ten to fifteen cents for the produce. The buyer, a jobber, who ships and sells the produce to a wholesaler, gets twenty-five cents. The wholesaler sells to a retailer at fifty cents—and the consumer buys the produce for $1.

Take an example of a small lettuce farmer in southern Texas. He sells his few acres of produce to a jobber who buys from many other farmers at the ten- to fifteen-cent level. The jobber combines his orders and ships to a regional wholesale house at twenty-five cents. That house buys from other jobbers, and can offer its customers almost anything in any quantity. The wholesale house distributes the produce for fifty cents to retail outlets. The customer often feels that someone is making too much because he's paying too much. But this isn't usually true.

Some try to beat the system by cutting out one or two of the middlemen. That's why co-ops are organized, why many farmers form their own jobber service, or, at the other end, why some small retailers buy directly from a jobber and eliminate the regional wholesalers. What you'd like to do with your cash gardening business is eliminate *all* of the middlemen and charge your customer retail prices. If this sounds impossible, read on.

HOW TO SELL?

By the Pound or the Item?

The trend is growing in this country to sell produce by the pound. I've seen lettuce, radishes, and grapefruit sold this way, rather than by the bunch or the item.

This seems the fairest way, for both buyer and seller, since the size and weight of fruits and vegetables can vary so much.

This is something to consider when setting your price policy.

Beating the System

The best example of the little guy who beats this system is a farm stand. You, the consumer, can see the produce growing in the fields behind the stand. It comes from the fields directly to the consumer with no middleman, no jobber, no wholesaler, and no expense. The prices are usually the same as or even higher than supermarket prices.

But don't think the local farm is making a bundle. It's difficult to raise crops and clear a profit. Most small farmers have to depend on several other sources of income to make ends meet. If they sell only what they raise, they can offer only a limited selection. Some stands expand, buying whatever they can't raise at wholesale so they can offer more variety. You've probably seen a small farm stand constantly expand over the years until it becomes a mini-shopping center, selling produce, cheese, baked goods, plants—some even have a butcher shop.

How You'll Operate

Your cash gardening business is in some ways the equivalent of the local farm stand. You'll eliminate the middlemen and sell directly to the consumer—in this case, your restaurant. You'll charge farm stand prices. The only difference is, you won't have trouble making ends meet, because gardening is a sideline for you. You won't have to branch out as the farm stands do, because you won't be depending on your gardening business for all your income. As you can see, the system I've developed gives you the best of both worlds. You can charge retail prices, but you don't have to share the money with anyone.

How Restaurants Buy

Let's look at your customer. How does your restaurant buy its fresh produce? In a large chain, the parent company often has its own purchasing department. Most individual restaurants buy from a wholesale company which takes their orders, buys at the wholesale market from jobbers, stocks and stores the produce, and then delivers along a truck route. Some of these companies have grown by stocking other food items and finally becoming full restaurant supply houses offering one-stop shopping (the one stop being their truck at the restaurant's back door). Some have anything and everything that a restaurant could want except customers: silverware, tables, furniture, dried flower arrangements—you name it. But most restaurants deal with several services: linen supply for napkins, tablecloths, aprons; bar supply for liquor and mixes. They may choose to deal with specialty companies such as those who supply nothing but fresh fish; or they may choose those who try to supply just about everything. The companies who specialize in one product usually offer better quality and are more expensive than the general suppliers. If there is a demand for their high-quality item, they will prosper. Let's see how *you,* as a new business owner, can fit into this scheme of things.

The Right Restaurant

As a specialty supplier of fresh home grown produce, you will want to search out the more discriminating restaurants. And believe me, things aren't always as they appear from the customer's viewpoint. I have found that the willingness to pay top dollar for fresh produce often depends as much on the inclination of the owner and head chef as on the type of restaurant. So, investigate the restaurant, then see if the produce buyer (the owner or chef) appreciates and desires fresh produce. Don't hesitate to approach a place that you think might be interested in homegrown produce or gourmet varieties. Go over chapter four again, and then go to it.

Let's go back to the question I posed at the beginning of this chapter. How much should you charge? Now that you've eliminated the middlemen, the jobbers, and wholesale restaurant suppliers, how can you possibly propose to a restaurant that he pay you at retail prices, or farm stand prices? He's probably expecting to save money by buying directly from you. How can you convince him to pay more than he did before? Here is the approach I recommend, and my justification for charging retail prices.

Your Approach

First, if you can find a restaurant that already uses farm-fresh produce and goes to a farm stand to get it, you'll save restaurant personnel trouble and expense by delivering it. No, even better than that, you'll wash it and put it in their cooler at no extra charge. You'll save them the time and effort of shopping, the kitchen help won't have to wash and clean the produce, and they won't have to pack and store it in their cooler. You'll do all this, and at no higher price than they'd pay for fresh produce at the farm stand.

Remember, you're not trying to supply the restaurant with all of its produce, but only with freshly picked items that it can't get elsewhere. And you just want to supply 20 or 30 percent of its needs.

Don't feel bashful about bringing up some of these strong points:

1. You are local, just as the restaurant is local.

2. You are just a little guy trying to make ends meet and start a small business, probably just like the restaurant owner started his, and you need a little help getting started.

3. Produce is just a small percentage of a restaurant's grocery bill, which itself is not one of the restaurant's major expenses. Since you only want 20 percent of its grocery business, how could that hurt the restaurant?

4. Think of the good will this will generate in the community, and all the favorable publicity. This surely will be written up in the local newspaper.

5. The advertising possibilities are endless: the restaurant can now offer as its slogan, "Eat Out Tonight From a Local Garden," or "We Serve Fresh Home grown Produce, Harvested Daily."

6. You'll charge farm stand prices—but you'll deliver.

7. There will be little or no waste in your produce.

You can think of lots of good sales points if you try. Practice on your spouse. (No, on second thought, don't do that. Your spouse may argue back.) Practice on yourself, posing all the questions a buyer might have and coming up with good answers. Always keep in mind just how important your selling price is. If the retail price of an item is $1, try to get it. If you have to settle for wholesale at fifty cents, you are going to have to produce twice as much to earn the same amount. Remember, though, that even if you produce twice as much, your profit will decrease. You'll be putting in twice as many hours, twice as many plants and seeds, twice as much fertilizer. You're not producing a huge harvest that would justify wholesale prices, so don't settle for wholesale price. *You're not in the wholesale business.*

Learn About Prices

It's a good idea to become familiar with current prices. Keep a list of those items you're thinking of growing and enter all local prices as you come across them. Get local supermarket and farm stand prices at least once a month. Then, as you make contacts in the business, inquire about the wholesale market and vendors' prices. They will all fluctuate as the seasons pass, and, more than likely, as the years go by. You don't want to charge last year's prices. Keep abreast of current prices in case your buyer questions anything. It would be very embarrassing to find out that lettuce is selling in the super-market for forty-nine cents and at the farm stand for fifty-nine cents while you are still charging seventy-nine cents. Conversely, you don't want to cheat yourself by undercharging.

If you rely on current wholesale prices to establish your sales price, you might want to subscribe to one of the government serv-ices. Many states, as well as the federal government, publish current wholesale prices for all kinds of goods. They are published either daily or weekly, depending on what state you live in. You can compare these with the supermarket and farm stand prices and establish your price with more certainty. If you don't have a farm stand nearby, check your supermarket for retail prices, then boost

U.S. Department of Agriculture publishes current lists of wholesale prices.

these by 10 to 20 percent. To get more information about what's available, look in the phone book under United States Government listing and your state offices for the Agriculture Department, and call them. You may also want to call your local county Extension Service agent, who can be a big help.

Measuring Vegetables

You are going to run across some unfamiliar units of measurement. We backyard gardeners think of lettuce in terms of heads, and count things like carrots as individual items. But buyers in the food business think of vegetables in terms of flats, lugs, cases, and hundredweights. Some items are sold by the pound, while others are sold by a unit of volume such as a packing crate. The size of the item will determine how many fit into a crate. Therefore the price per head can change drastically, depending on how many fit into the crate. Be careful when you hear that lettuce is forty-nine cents a head. Those may be very tiny heads, packed twenty-four to a crate, while yours may be large enough to be packed twelve to a crate.

To further complicate the matter, terms are different across the country, so a flat or crate is not always the same. Learn them in your area.

The food business also has a complete vocabulary to describe the size and quality of produce. Quality in this case refers not to taste, but to looks. Sometimes they go by Grade A, B, or C, or Premium, Best, and Standard. Jot these terms down as you hear them, and don't be afraid to ask about unfamiliar ones, so you'll know how to compare your "perfect produce" with the trade standards. Keep in mind that yours may not always look as uniform as the commercial varieties, but it sure is going to taste better.

Taste Comes Last

The rapid expansion of supermarket produce departments, coupled with the demand for perfect-*looking* fruits and vegetables, has pressured the American farmer into producing a vegetable that ships well and looks good. Unfortunately, taste has had to take a back seat. We have no one to blame but ourselves, as we customers want only the best-looking produce. We don't want blemishes or soft spots, so the outer surface has to be tough enough to withstand mechanical picking, rolling along conveyor belts, tumbling into containers, shipping cross-country, and being stored for long periods of time, all without dents or bruises.

Keep mentioning to your buyer how good your vegetables taste, how fresh they are. Just think, they will be in his restaurant cooler within an hour or two of harvest. Absolutely no one, not even the local farm stands, can offer that. If you need an extra sales pitch, talk up the fact that you have something unique and different, something no one else has.

Out-of-Season Prices

By keeping a monthly list of supermarket, farm stand, and wholesale prices, you can take advantage of any out-of-season produce you have. The law of supply and demand still prevails in the marketplace. When every home gardener has tomatoes coming out of his ears, he won't buy them at the supermarket. Local farmers will also have plenty at this time, and what's the result? Prices drop. Conversely, at the beginning and end of each season, the supply is low. Since the demand is still there, prices go up. If you work to have a small harvest at the beginning and end of each season (see chapter sixteen), that extra work will pay off with higher returns.

What if your buyer refuses to pay more than he does to the restaurant supply house? This is what you hoped to avoid, but all is not lost. First, ask for a copy of the supplier's current price list. If necessary, photocopy it and return the original. Then ask for a little time to think it over. This will give you a chance to find another customer before you decide to take less than farm stand prices.

Farm stand prices are usually 10 to 20 percent above supermarket prices. A good part of the country doesn't have farm stands anymore. Most people live in the suburbs, with little open space devoted to agriculture. So even if you live in the city, don't be confused when I mention farm stand prices. They are the slightly higher prices that people are willing to pay for farm-fresh produce. Most people assume that farm stand prices should be cheaper— after all, they grow the produce right there, and how much does it cost to pick it and put it on the counter? But unless the farm stand is just a sideline for the family, you will find the owner charging whatever the market will bear. And you'll probably feel the same way when you start raising and delivering your own home-grown produce.

What if you can't find another restaurant to buy your produce at farm stand prices? What financial loss will you be taking if you go back to your original customer? Since the restaurant supply house buys wholesale and has to make a little profit, it is selling somewhere between wholesale and retail. Because of the high cost of delivery, stocking large quantities of everything available, and the expense of taking phone orders and delivering the next day, the restaurant houses usually charge between 10 and 20 percent below retail level. If farm stand prices are 10 to 20 percent above retail or supermarket prices, you wouldn't be losing out completely.

For example, at a retail $1 level, the farm stand would be $1.10 to $1.20 while the restaurant supply house would charge between eighty and ninety cents. So if you had to settle for the lower prices you would be getting an average of thirty cents less on a $1 item. Although that's a big difference, it's not as bad as running a wholesale business at the fifty-cent level.

So there's your choice. Sell at wholesale in large quantities at fifty cents; deliver at restaurant supply prices at eighty-five cents; sell at retail of $1, or try for the top dollar of farm-fresh at $1.10-$1.20. Assuming your costs to raise and deliver will vary from fifteen to twenty-five cents, here's a chart on your potential profit.

Keep in mind your main selling point is fresh, home-grown. You might even ask to look at what is being delivered so you can show how much fresher and better looking your harvest will be, and how much less waste there will be for the restaurant owner.

As a final argument, you might suggest to the owner or chef, "Let's try it at farm stand prices, and if, after a month or so, you don't feel you're getting full value, we can talk about some adjustments."

It's very much in your interest to start at the highest price possible.

YOUR PROFITS

	Wholesale	Restaurant Supply House	Retail	Farm Stand
If you sell at	.50	.85	1.00	1.15
Your costs are	.20	.20	.20	.20
Your profit is	.30	.65	.80	.95
Increase over wholesale profit is		215%	265%	315%

These are general averages over the whole country. In many states, we found a trend for restaurant supply houses to charge the same or more than the local retail supermarket prices. This means that you will have less persuading to do to collect farm stand prices from your restaurant.

Chapter 7
Delivery and Collection

$ This is a key chapter, because it covers some of the most important techniques you must learn to stay in business and make a profit. I'll talk about some tricks of the trade, too. All of the information in this chapter is based on first-hand experience: my own and others who have tried this method. These techniques have worked for me; they'll work for you as well.

When to Deliver

How often, on what days, and at what time you should deliver your produce depends as much on the restaurant's schedule as your own. As soon as you've thought it over, meet with the owner or manager and discuss a permanent schedule. He might want the head chef or salad chef to sit in on this talk.

For your benefit as well as the restaurant's, you should deliver at least twice, and possibly three times, per week. A lot depends on how large your operation is. Will an entire order—all you can harvest—fit in your vehicle with one trip? How far do you have to travel to deliver?

Don't get talked into delivering only once a week if this is your only customer. For vegetables to be harvested at their peak, a week is too long a time between harvests. A restaurant will also have to store most of a full week's harvest for several days, thereby negating your biggest selling point: fresh produce delivered within hours of its harvest. That's your most important advantage; don't lose it by opting for an "easy" weekly delivery schedule. Remember, to a commercial grower, a vegetable's most important quality is not flavor, but shipping and keeping qualities. The restaurant has hired you to get something different, varieties that have the flavor and freshness that can't be found in the commercial market.

Making a Schedule

Talk over with the owner the number of meals to be served and when. Some restaurants are closed Monday or Tuesday and have little business on Sunday. Any produce left over from the weekend would be wilted, definitely not top quality. You'd want to deliver to these customers on the morning of the day they reopen, and again on Friday morning for the weekend trade.

Set up a delivery schedule so your produce is used up in two or three days at the most. This should be easy if you don't get piggy and try to furnish more than 30 percent of your customer's needs.

The typical restaurant does most of its business over the weekend. If it's successful, its business during the week should also be fairly uniform. Schedule your delivery for the busiest day, as long as there is one good day following. For example, if Saturday night is the busiest, Friday night next, then Sunday afternoon, then Wednesday evening, closed Monday, slow on Tuesday, I'd try to set up a Wednesday-Friday or Wednesday-Saturday delivery schedule. I wouldn't go to three deliveries a week unless that restaurant had a fairly big weekday clientele. Then I'd set up a Tuesday-Thursday-Saturday schedule. Of course, you can stagger your harvest by picking lightly early in the week and heavily (everything in sight that's big enough) on weekends. Despite all your scheduling, Mother Nature occasionally makes her presence known. Just when you've picked all beans in sight, thinking you'll have plenty more by next week, she'll keep Old Man Sun behind a curtain of clouds and you'll get five days of showers. Result: no beans for next week. If this possibility is explained to the owner, he won't plan menus around your harvest.

Don't take orders for specific quantities and items. If you do, you will have to grow twice as much and wind up throwing away half your produce, or rushing around looking for another market to whom you can sell your surplus. Just be sure your customer understands your agreement: he'll take whatever you have ready to harvest each week.

When to Deliver

Next question is when to deliver: morning or afternoon? A lot will depend on *your* habits and your job, if you're working. Do you like to get up early, or do you snooze until nine every morning? You might as well run your business to suit yourself, if that's possible. A typical harvest will take two to four hours, so keep that in mind when you make up your schedule. Don't say you'll be there at 9 A.M. if you hate to get up in the morning; your business will turn into drudgery. It's better to choose a more reasonable hour and enjoy your work.

However, you must consider the heat of the sun. Produce wilts fast on a hot, sunny day, even in the shade. Try to harvest and deliver before or after the heat of the day. In the spring and fall that's not as important, and some of the summer vegetables such as tomatoes and eggplants aren't affected by daytime heat. If you wait until after the hottest hours you'll have to rush to harvest and deliver before 6 P.M. Most restaurants start preparing the evening vegetables by mid-afternoon, and this would be far too late for them, so talk it over with the chef.

The best plan may be to pick all morning and deliver around noontime. Keep everything in the shade, wetted down, and get it into the cooler quickly once you're there. Even if the restaurant is busy with the noon meal, the kitchen help is used to receiving deliveries all day long. There should be no problem, especially if you're willing to unload and store your delivery.

Of course, you rooster types who have your harvest all ready to deliver by 10 A.M. have the ideal situation. You won't get in anybody's way, and you'll have the rest of the day to lie in your hammock, if you don't have to rush to your job.

Stick to Schedule

Whether it's morning or afternoon, twice a week or three times, don't veer from your schedule. Always be on time, rain or shine, sick or well, large harvest or small. Be the one person that they can say is truly dependable. It may not seem so important to you now, but your regularity will help guarantee you future business there. The owner will get used to your fresh produce and look forward to it; he'll even look forward to each delivery. You're something out of the past—an honest-to-goodness dirt farmer who loves his work and is proud of it.

How to Deliver

When you drive up to the loading dock to make your delivery, your harvest should look like something out of *Successful Farming*. If you have an old red Chevy pickup and wear overalls, everyone will know what you have in the back. But if you don't have all those colorful accoutrements, you'd better have a good-looking harvest. It must be washed and sparkling clean, sorted and packed, weighed or counted, and, most important, arranged to look its best. Each time you pack for delivery, pretend some famous magazine will be there to take a picture of your harvest. Move quickly once your harvest is packed so it doesn't have time to wilt or fade.

Who to See

Make a point of checking in with the owner if at all possible. Never do business with the busboy, kitchen helper, or potato peeler. Get the owner, manager, or head chef to look over and accept your delivery before you unload and store your produce.

A very important step in your delivery operation is to get to know the important people who work there and what their responsibilities are. Do this without taking a lot of time or asking a lot of questions. Don't stand around talking to anyone, not even the owner. You might think these people are ever so friendly and interested in your business when in reality the boss might be too shy or polite to say he's got work to do, or the cook should be working but will have a smoke and shoot the breeze with anyone who comes along. If that anyone is you and the boss sees it happen more than once, guess who's going to be out of business?

Learn Who's Who

How do you get to know who's who, then? You keep your eyes open and mouth shut. It's often been said, "You won't learn much while your mouth is working." Look for the person who takes charge, gives orders, seems responsible, and looks after your produce. Ask the boss or head chef to introduce you to the person who's responsible for putting away your produce.

Get to know that person by observing his habits. Is he careful in handling fresh produce, or do you think he would do better in the meat cooler? Is this just a job to him, or does he seem interested in and proud of his work? Watch his reaction to your beautiful, carefully arranged produce. If he tastes fresh items, exclaiming over their color or crispness, you've got a friend. If not, you'd better do the handling yourself. You've already brought it from the garden, washed and cleaned it, packed, loaded, and unloaded it; it's not much farther to the cooler. If you put it away, you'll know it's done right. Some people will say, "That's too much work; you're making my job harder than necessary." My answer is, if you take pride in your harvest and want to be successful in business, you'll be willing to do a little extra.

Unloading

If you have a truck or station wagon with lots of room so the produce looks picturesque when you drive up, don't unload until the boss sees it. Park out of the sun, leave all your windows open, and don't let it stay there long.

If your produce is packed in tightly or piled in layers in your car trunk, unload first. Put everything in the shade, attractively arranged, and then get the boss. Keep a filled sprinkler can handy to freshen up your produce. Nothing is more tempting than freshly picked vegetables sparkling with water droplets. Your best-looking produce should be the most prominently displayed, keeping the most colorful vegetables up front. Bring your camera along once in a while and take the owner's picture alongside your harvest. You'll have a friend for life.

Incidentally, you don't have to get the boss to come to the loading dock to show him the produce. Often you'll pass the office, or he'll be in the kitchen supervising. If you're walking toward the cooler, it's a great opportunity to say, "How do you like this crate of carrots?" Or take some parsley right into his office and say, "I'm so proud of this, I just had to show it to you." Of course you don't want to do this very often; just enough so you and your produce aren't forgotten.

What if you can't find the top man, or no one's available at the moment? If they say, "Just unload it; we'll look at it later," you have no choice but to go ahead. But even then, don't leave until you see everything safely put away in the cooler.

Loading Dock Blues

Most people would be very happy if someone told them, "Just leave it here on the loading dock. We'll put it away." This could be one of the most disastrous mistakes you'll ever make. I did it once and I'll never do it again. It cost me $85 worth of fresh, delicate leaf lettuce, along with an assortment of other vegetables. It was a brutally hot, sticky day. After four hours of harvesting I was ready for a nice, tall, cold one with lots of foam. Everyone at the restaurant was too busy to come, and the busboy said, "Just stack it over here and I'll put it away as soon as I finish my lunch."

Well, I heard that later—much later—the owner came upon the saddest looking wilted lettuce and limp carrots he'd ever seen. I almost lost my best customer. Naturally, he was angry with the busboy who forgot everything until mid-afternoon. But I'm sure he couldn't help thinking, "Why am I paying top dollar for this?"

How to Store It

You should see that the produce is put away in the cooler, and that it is properly put away. Don't let anyone put your flats of lettuce on the cooler floor where someone will probably stack crates of grapefruit on top of them. Remember the Peter Principle, "If there's any chance your produce may get crushed, it will," or "If only one flat gets lost in the corner until it molds, it'll be yours."

The point is that you could say goodbye at the loading dock, but you'd probably be saying goodbye to your business before very long. If you want to be successful, make sure everything is not only grown and harvested in the best way, but that it gets delivered and put away properly.

The Cooler

You might as well stop right now and learn a little bit about the cooler and how it's used. Every restaurant has a walk-in refrigerated room for storing vegetables and fruit. Some store meat and dairy products in the same room if they have only one. But watch out—it may be too cold for tender varieties of vegetables.

First, to ease your fears about going into a cooler alone, the door can be opened from the inside, despite any late-night movies you may see on TV. The light will also have a switch or pull cord on the inside. Depending on your particular restaurant, the cooler may have neatly stacked shelves with produce arranged by categories, or the food may be piled wherever there's an empty space. Watch out—this is a place where your fragile lettuce will wind up on the bottom of a stack or be pushed into an unused corner. Another warning sign is containers of leftover food lying about. I'm not suggesting you start reorganizing the shelves (although I've done that at times), but keep your eyes open and observe how the food is stored and handled. It will help you in knowing what to grow, how to best pack and store it, and the type of restaurant you're dealing with.

The cooler is a wonderful place. You see all sorts of tempting out-of-season fruits, berries, and vegetables. One word of caution: don't snitch anything. It doesn't belong to you. Even if you see others sampling, don't you do it. Once seen, you'll never be trusted again. Even if someone offers me something, I always say, "No, thank you." You never know if they're supposed to be offering it.

Leftovers?

While you're in the cooler, see whether your last week's delivery is all gone. If not, maybe you're bringing too much too fast, in which case it will spoil and have to be thrown out. Despite your protests, this will reflect on your business. You could easily say, "That's not my responsibility; they buy it—let them worry about using it." Not true! You want to establish a relationship in which they're happy to see you arrive, glad to get your produce, willing to pay top dollar for it, and willing to take whatever you bring them.

This almost insures the success of your business. There aren't many businesses that sell everything they make or stock. The rest is waste, overage, or unsaleable at the end of the season. Many truck farmers can't sell anywhere near half of what they raise. I've seen huge piles of eggplant, tomatoes, and cabbage rotting in the fields because their roadside stands or normal markets couldn't sell them especially at the peak of the season.

In most businesses you must plan on this overage and adjust your prices accordingly. But with cash gardening, you get top dollar for *all* that you can raise. Since the secret is to furnish the restaurant with only 10 to 30 percent of *its* needs, it won't be dependent on your delivery. Yet it can incorporate any variation of your harvest into its menu for that week.

You can see now how important it was to discuss all this with the restaurant owner or chef at the very beginning. You might have to remind him that you are able to provide him with such good produce at such reasonable prices only because he can take all you raise each week. You still have to grow those things the restaurant wants, needs, and can use, and in reasonable quantities so it doesn't become over-burdened with too much of one thing. Remember the fundamentals of a cash garden: you only want to deliver about one-fifth of the restaurant's needs. Then virtually nothing can ever go wrong.

Offer Suggestions

Since you want the cooks to use your fresh produce first, keep an eye on how fast they use it. Just a friendly reminder that last week's beets are still in the cooler will alert the chef that a slight menu change is needed to use them up. That protects you, especially if you have a lot more coming to maturity at home. I've even suggested special dishes or menus for using a particular vegetable when I'm expecting a bumper crop in the next few weeks. This helps to ensure that you sell everything you raise. All you have to say is, "Green beans will be coming in strong for the next three weeks or so, but carrots will be slow for another month."

Rules to Remember

Some general ground rules to keep in mind:

- Don't gossip; never complain about the weather or the cost of living.
- Always be positive.
- Be cheerful, friendly, and have a smile and a good word for all. They'll get to look forward to your visits.
- Be as nice a person as your produce.
- Never smoke in or near the restaurant, even if others do.
- Keep your truck or car clean and neat: it's an extension of your business.
- Have something nice to say about your harvest each week: "Look how nice these carrots are;" "Try some of this fresh spinach;" "Wait until you see the Swiss chard next week."

If you can follow these rules, the staff will look forward to your deliveries, the chef will have a better attitude toward your produce, and the owner will be happy to pay you each week. They'll feel that, between you and your produce, they're getting a bargain.

Records to Keep

What delivery records should you keep? Only enough to tell you how much of what and at what price was delivered each week. It can be a simple itemized list, showing how many units or pounds of each vegetable were delivered each time and at what price. Should you lump all leaf lettuce together or should you have a separate line for each variety—Ruby, buttercrunch, oak leaf? If the restaurant doesn't want it, and they usually don't, why bother? It's just a lot of paperwork and extra figuring. If they all sell for the same price, lump them together. The only reason to keep more detailed records is to help in planning next year.

Here is my typical weekly delivery list:

DATE _____ SQUARE FOOT GARDENING
Pheasant Run Farm
Old Field, NY 11733

10 bunches Carrots @ 89¢ = 8.90
23 # Tomatoes @ 69¢ = 15.87
4 qts ch. Tom. @ 1⁴⁹ = 5.96
8 bunches Sw. Ch @ .59 = 4.72
4 bunches Parsley @ .49 = 1.96
18 heads Leaf lettuce @ .79 = 14.22
12 heads Cos lettuce @ .69 = 8.28
14 # Bell Peppers @ .59 = 8.26
15 each Cucumbers @ 25¢ = 3.75
          Total $ ~~25.92~~
                   $ 71.92

To further simplify it and keep costs down, I use bank deposit slips.
They have lines for the restaurant's name and the date, and all the lines
below are ideal for listing the varieties of produce. I keep a carbon
copy for myself in a different color. I don't know if the banks would
appreciate my suggesting this, but it seems a small expenditure compared to all they spend on advertising to get you to think that their
bank is different from the others.

The only difference I've ever found among banks is that some have clean, simple deposit slips in pretty colors, while others have very cluttered, dull ones.

LIST EACH CHECK SEPARATELY BY BANK NUMBER		
~~CHECKS~~	~~DOLLARS~~	~~CENTS~~
Date ——		
10 heads	leaf lettuce	
	@.79	7.90
5 #	Bell Peppers	
	@.59	2.95
4 qts.	Ch. Tomatoes	
	@1.69	6.76
8 ea.	Cucumbers @	
	.25	2.00
4 bu.	Parsley @ 49	1.96
	TOTAL $21	57
	$21.57	
PLEASE FORWARD TOTAL TO REVERSE SIDE.		

Invest in a small pocket calculator to do your addition and multiplication so you can present a totaled delivery slip as soon as you arrive. Now for the big step ....

How to Collect in Cash

Since you've already agreed with the owner that you can collect upon completion of delivery, it shouldn't be any trouble. But be alert for snags and make sure the first time goes smoothly. Don't be put off by any excuses, especially the first time. This is the crux of your business; if you can't collect every week and have to start giving credit, you're starting a new business—banking. **Don't do it,** even for one week.

Once your harvest is unloaded, checked, or at least seen by the owner, make sure it's put away properly and then collect your money. You might ask the owner, "Who should I see for payment when you're not here?" while you hand him his copy of the delivery slip. That's a subtle way of saying, "I'd like to get paid now for my delivery." If you say, "Here's your copy of the delivery slip," he might say, "Thank you," and go on his way, leaving you on the loading dock wondering what's next, or chasing him down the hallway into the kitchen. If you're lucky, he'll say, "You can see Jane over here each week." Now you've got a specific person to collect from, and you don't have to bother the boss every time you deliver.

Here's the payoff. The chef gets the vegetables and you get the cash.

But what happens if you're not lucky? Well, in most cases, if you're dealing with a friendly, honest person, you'll have no trouble getting paid. But if the boss tries to put you off, what do you say to the fifty-eight excuses he'll try to give you for not paying you right away? Give him a reply that responds directly to his excuse. Here are some examples.

EXCUSES	YOUR ANSWERS
"My cashier is out sick."	"Whoever is handy; the register is O.K."
"We're out of cash right now."	"I don't mind waiting."
"We're a little low this week."	"Everyone seems to be low this week."
"We only pay bills once a month."	"This agreement is based on weekly payments, remember?"
"I'm very busy right now."	"I'll be out of your way in a flash."
"I can't handle money now; I'm cooking."	"Whom should I ask instead?"
"Can you come back later?"	"I'll be busy at my garden."
"How about next week?"	"I couldn't let it go a whole week."
"Would you mind waiting until next week?"	"Normally I would, but I can't this week."
"Can't do it now."	"I kept my part of the bargain —your vegetables are all unloaded and stored."
"Impossible."	"Nothing is impossible if you want to do it."
"No."	"You'll have to tell me why, since that's unfair."

Add to your response, "You know, we agreed to weekly payments." This will gently remind him that he's going back on his word, and that you're aware of it, so he won't try this again next week.

Try Being Sympathetic

You could also try being sympathetic: "I know it's tough to make ends meet these days," or "It must be very hard to run a successful restaurant," *but* "I'm a gardener, not a banker. That's why we agreed to payment upon delivery."

Then try getting some sympathy: "I'm just a little guy trying to make ends meet;" "I can't compete with big companies, but I can produce better vegetables;" "My business and expenses are all cash, so I have to get paid weekly to stay in business;" "I can't offer credit, compete with the big companies, and still give you top produce at reasonable prices."

Or try to appeal to his sense of fellowship: "We're both local people who deal in food. We both take pride in producing the best-looking, best-tasting food around; we could be helping each other toward a common goal—to run our businesses efficiently and make a profit."

With all that logic and these good arguments, how can he refuse you?

Chapter 8

Even More Cash

$ Let me tell you a secret. It's how to make even more cash from your square foot garden:

Don't throw anything away.

Let me tell you another secret:

Don't concentrate so on not throwing anything away that you lose sight of what you're in business to do, and that's to raise quality vegetables and sell them at top prices.

Now let me explain about not throwing anything away. For example, leftovers. What happens if you have too much lettuce to deliver to your restaurant, far more than it can use? If you leave that lettuce for an extra week, it may get too large and start bolting to seed. As a good gardener, you'll be able to tell if it has to be cut this week. Then it can either go into your family's kitchen, or those of your friends.

Or you might decide to sell some of your leftovers. You could make an arrangement with a neighbor or even other businesses to take the extras whenever they're available. It's not a good idea to take your seconds to your main buyer. Take him only your very best, even if it means you can't supply as much as he would like. You want to stick to premium standards with him.

Many communities set up a farmers' market one or several days a week, and some cash gardeners have found that taking produce there works out quite well. Anything that's left over after they deliver to their prime buyer is sold at the farmers' market. But you must always ask yourself how much your time is worth. Can you realize the maximum return in dollars per hour by sitting at a local market waiting for customers to come? Don't forget to figure in the expenses of getting there, the fees you'll have to pay, the cost of bags and scales, and any other costs.

If you have a regular job, you could only do this on weekends, and then you might be too busy to attend.

Alternatives

There are other things you can do with your leftovers, and you might want to consider some of them. Can they be stored, dried, or frozen? If so, they could be sold at a later date, or saved for your own use.

Of course, you could always give them to the needy through a local church or charitable organization that feeds or distributes food to the underprivileged. Get a receipt for the amount, multiply that by the fair market value, and you've got yourself a dandy tax deduction that means real dollars to you.

As a last resort, you can always take them to the compost pile to help enrich next year's crop.

Undersized Produce

In trying to sell everything possible, you might also try to sell your undersized produce. When deciding what is "undersized," you should discuss this with your buyer. If you have all medium-size heads of lettuce for a couple of weeks, he won't object, providing you lower the per-head price. When you have extra-large heads, their price will naturally go up. You can see that if you were using the normal commercial standards of a flat or crate of lettuce, the price per crate would be very different than the price per head as the size of the head changes. When sixteen heads of a large size fit into one crate, the price per head will certainly be higher than twenty-four heads fitting into the same size crate, but the price per crate will be the same. I think it's always better to base your prices on a per-head or per-item base. The same would apply to carrots, beets, and anything that can be harvested at several different sizes.

I remember one restaurant owner who, by negotiating a special deal, bought leftovers and undersized vegetables from me at less than half price. Since he was more interested in economy than in quality, he began to ask for more of the cheaper commodities, and after several weeks, he told me, "We'll take undersized only. We don't want any more of the select." I had just lost my prime business.

Chinese cucumbers like these are easy to raise and bring a good price.

TRY GOURMET VEGETABLES

For top-dollar profits, try raising gourmet vegetables.

They are just as easy to grow as the more common varieties, and they bring in extra dollars.

Make certain, first, that you have a market for them, someone who needs and appreciates the unusual varieties, and is willing to pay the extra price for them. Be sure, too, to know the volume of them that will be purchased.

You may have to search to find the seeds. Most major seed companies offer a limited number, and specialty mail order companies offer a good choice. Here are a few to consider:

Carrots: Look for varieties that produce the earliest crop, long, thin, or round shapes.

Lettuce: Try corn salad or rocket salad, and look for varieties of leaf and buttercrunch types that are especially suited for spring forcing, overwintering, or heat-resistant, to give you a year-round crop.

Cucumbers: Concentrate on the long, thin varieties from France, China, and Japan.

Radishes: Look for the unusual shapes of many European and Oriental varieties.

Also try: Celeriac, red chicory, witloof chicory or Belgian endive, Finocchio (fennel), cress, mustard, and spinach.

One Exception

There is one time when you should sell your undersized vegetables and that is at the end of the growing season. You can protect and hold over any cool weather crops, but they grow very slowly in the cold weather. Most gardeners would rather harvest what they can and close up the garden for the winter.

If you have enough of one thing, it doesn't matter if it's undersized, in fact it may then be considered as gourmet or petit and command a higher price. You could even sell all your green tomatoes for a special recipe. I've seen tiny carrots, miniature bibb lettuce, small eggplant, peppers, beets, scallions, Japanese turnip, and radishes all sold at a premium price because of their size. But you have to have enough of these to make it worthwhile for the restaurant.

How to Charge

Usually the price per pound is about twice the price for normal size. That reflects the extra labor and material involved in such small sizes. Of course, since the items are less than one-half size, the buyer gets three times as many items for that price.

For example, a cellophane package of ten medium-size carrots (one pound) might retail for 59¢, or 6¢ each. Another one-pound package would contain about thirty tiny carrots and retail for $1.29, or 4¢ each. If those were farm-fresh, arranged in small bunches with the tops on, the price would be double that.

So, for undersized vegetables you could safely double the normal price per pound. This will work equally well with all vegetables including lettuce. Just remember to weigh the lettuce when it's not dripping wet.

Don't Try Too Hard

One word of caution: If you put too much effort into selling your seconds or undersized vegetables, your main business, which needs your full attention, may suffer. You can't be scurrying around trying to sell things at half-price and neglect your main business.

No Handouts

You may also find a lot of friends and neighbors looking for freebies, and pretty soon you'll start feeling obligated to them. The same thing happens when you sell to them. It's very difficult to collect money for something that your friends, neighbors, or your family would expect to get free from a gardener. That's one reason why I invented square foot gardening. I realized that the old-fashioned single-row garden was producing too much all at once, and so there was a surplus to get rid of. Although the square foot system staggers the harvest through controlled planting, everyone still clings to the incorrect notion that all gardeners have an overabundance of produce which they can give away.

Two Goals

Keep in mind that the two most important goals for your cash gardening business are to grow a top quality product and to deliver consistently every week. When you're striving to grow a perfect crop, you don't want anything to interfere with that, especially the first year or two. That's why I caution everyone who's just getting started: don't get caught up in what you're going to do with your undersized, leftovers, or seconds. If you can't eat them, and don't have close friends who aren't looking for continual freebies, put everything in the compost pile, where they'll help you with next year's crop. Learn from your experience how much to plant.

Of course, there are ways of stretching out your season and holding things so they'll last a little longer. For example, if you're getting too much lettuce coming to size all at once, cover half your crop with shade film and stretch out your harvest for another week or so. But again, if you hold the lettuce back from rapid growth, the taste may lose some of its quality. You may be sacrificing your reputation and business for twenty or thirty heads of lettuce.

For your first year, concentrate on growing the best produce you can and delivering only the perfect vegetables to your prime cash customer. Don't worry about anything else that first year. Get your routine under control, and establish a consistent record with your buyer for bringing him the absolute best at a reasonable price.

Once your business is established, you can try some of these suggestions, but keep in mind always your main goal of raising and selling most of your produce to one or two main buyers without getting sidetracked by several incidental ventures. Your major profit will come from this main business.

Chapter 9
Rules and Regulations

 The bad news is that you'll have to keep some business records and fill out some forms if you go into square foot gardening to make money.

The good news is that you won't have to keep many records, and some of them, instead of being headaches, will enable you to save some money by reducing your income taxes.

You'll save yourself a lot of trouble in the months ahead if you'll just decide that there are a few records to be kept and forms to be filled out, then find out what they are, and start work on them.

Because laws differ from state to state, and county to county, and even town to town, I can't tell you what paperwork you'll be required to do in your community.

But I can tell you how to go about finding out.

Call the Right People

First of all be sure you call the right people at the very beginning. Keep a record of your phone conversations, and make sure to get each person's name, title, and telephone number. Ask him to mail you copies of the pertinent rules and regulations so you have them on file.

I like to end a conversation by asking, "Is there anything else you think I should know?" In that way, you sometimes elicit a suggestion that you might not have gotten had you tried to determine everything yourself. You may even be referred to another department. After all, these people are experts at their jobs; they may know what you're looking for better than you yourself do.

The first thing to find out is whether you can conduct a small business from your home. I would suggest you start with your county agricultural agent. You'll find him in the county listings of your phone book under Extension Service.

Tell him exactly what you plan to do and ask if any rules or regulations or zoning laws prohibit you from raising fresh vegetables in your backyard and selling them to a restaurant. Then ask what records you should keep and whether there are any reports, permits, fees, or licenses required.

In most cases you'll find you get a go-ahead, provided there's no continuous or heavy flow of customers in and out of your home, you're not delivering across the state line, you're not displaying or selling your produce on public land (on the street or in a parking lot), and you're not selling living plants still growing in soil.

You're selling to a restaurant, which in effect is reselling the food, and because you're selling food for consumption, most state sales tax laws don't apply. But call your state sales tax agency anyway, just to make sure.

Most towns don't require a permit or license, either, because you're a small home business selling locally, and aren't involved in the public marketplace. Call your town clerk or zoning office for advice.

Income Taxes

Income tax is a totally different story. If you earn a profit, the federal government wants to know about it. Your state does, too, if it has a state income tax. So you have to keep a few records. This is not complicated or elaborate—in fact it's nothing more than you're probably doing right now with your personal expenses. I've found that if you pay all your business expenses by check, you'll have a perfect record for your income tax deductions. You might even want to open a separate checking account (try to get one of those free ones some banks offer from time to time) and write all your garden expense checks on that account.

To keep things even more simple, deposit all your income from the business in that checking account, and you'll have all the records you need in one small, convenient book. Start a new book every calendar year, and tuck away the old one with the yearly federal income tax return copy that you keep.

The only other things you have to keep are receipts to back up your expense claims for all the bills you've paid. The Internal Revenue Service can demand to see a record for any payment over $25. That seems to be the magic number; for anything under that amount, they seem to trust you.

Your Deductions

Keep in mind that you can deduct many expenses from your income. In fact, "any reasonable legal business expense" means every penny that you spend for the business, connected with the business, or because of the business. Here's a rule of thumb to help you decide: ask yourself, "If I didn't have this business, would I have spent that money?" If the answer is "No," you can usually classify that item as a business expense. Think about travel, for example. Visiting public gardens or arboretums to talk with their experts about certain vegetables; any trip to the county agricultural agent to discuss your business; certainly all your trips to see prospective clients and, later, your restaurant deliveries—all the travel you do to sell your produce or scout out new ideas is tax-deductible.

When you're on those trips, whether they be short hops or overnight excursions, you should keep records of your mileage and anything you spend. This should include lunches or dinners, whom you took to dinner, and what you discussed there. Sounds complicated, but it's not, particularly if you paid by check or credit card. Even if you paid with cash, you can get a receipt from the restaurant; on the back, jot down who you were with and what you discussed.

I've found it's very easy to write a check, made out to cash, for that exact amount; then that expenditure is recorded in your checkbook. The same applies when you buy gas for your car, pay for any car repairs, or incur parking fees. While you're on your trip, you might make out a simple "trip ticket" which lists all of these expenses. When you get home you can write a check made out to cash, for the total amount. Now you have a complete record of the total money spent on the trip with a matching check stub, all ready for your income tax records.

Many Expenses

There are, of course, many other expenses associated with your small business. Some are things you'll need for your garden, such as supplies, tools, plants and seeds; but others will be normal household expenses that will become eligible as business expenses. For example, a portion of your telephone, water, sewerage, and garbage fees can be charged against the business. If you use a room in your house, or space in your garage to conduct your business and store records, a portion of your heat and electric bills can be written off against the business. The easiest way to do this is to set up a chart using categories found in the Standard IRS Schedule C, which is used for small businesses. Then go through your personal checkbook and deduct those items that apply to that room. To determine the percentage, figure the approximate size of that room against the approximate size of your house; use that percentage to figure the deduction for heat and electricity. If you hire someone to watch the children while you're delivering, that, too, is a deductible fee. Make sure you keep records of amounts paid, and to whom, to back up anything you put down on Schedule C. Don't forget any office, gardening, harvesting, or delivery equipment that you buy.

If you are conscientious about your record-keeping, filling out Schedule C will be a very easy task at income tax time.

SCHEDULE C (Form 1040)	**Profit or (Loss) From Business or Profession** (Sole Proprietorship)
Department of the Treasury Internal Revenue Service (O)	Partnerships, Joint Ventures, etc., Must File Form 1065. ► Attach to Form 1040 or Form 1041. ► See Instructions for Schedule C

Name of proprietor _____ Soc

A Main business activity (see Instructions) ►_____ Product or Service ►

B Business name and address ►................................... **C** Employer ID number

D Method(s) used to value closing inventory:
   (1) ☐ Cost   (2) ☐ Lower of cost or market   (3) ☐ Other (attach explanation)
E Accounting method: (1) ☐ Cash   (2) ☐ Accrual   (3) ☐ Other (specify) ►.....................
F Was there any change in determining quantities, costs, or valuations between opening and closing inventory?. . .
   If "Yes," attach explanation.
G Did you deduct expenses for an office in your home? . . . .

Part I   Income

1 a	Gross receipts or sales	1a
b	Less: Returns and allowances	1b
c	Subtract line 1b from line 1a and enter the balance here	1c
2	Cost of goods sold and/or operations (from Part III, line 8)	2
3	Subtract line 2 from line 1c and enter the **gross profit** here . . .	3
4 a	Windfall Profit Tax Credit or Refund received in 1984 (see Instructions) . . .	4a
b	Other income	4b
5	Add lines 3, 4a, and 4b. This is the **gross income** . . . . ►	5

Part II   Deductions

6 Advertising		23 Repairs	
7 Bad debts from sales or services (Cash method taxpayers, see Instructions)		24 Supplies (not included in Part III below)	
		25 Taxes (Do not include Windfall Profit Tax here. See line 29) . .	
8 Bank service charges.			
9 Car and truck expenses		26 Travel and entertainment . . .	
10 Commissions		27 Utilities and telephone	
11 Depletion		28 a Wages . . .	
12 Depreciation and Section 179 deduction from Form 4562 (not included in Part III below).		b Jobs credit	
		c Subtract line 28b from 28a . .	
13 Dues and publications		29 Windfall Profit Tax withheld in 1984	
14 Employee benefit programs . . .		30 Other expenses (specify):	
15 Freight (not included in Part III below) .		a	
16 Insurance		b	
17 Interest on business indebtedness . .		c	
18 Laundry and cleaning		d	
19 Legal and professional services . .		e	
20 Office expense.		f	
21 Pension and profit-sharing plans . .		g	
22 Rent on business property . . .		h	
		i	

How to Organize

Here's another suggestion: set up twelve large envelopes labeled "Bills to be Paid," one for each month. I save used ones from the mail. At the end of the month, pay your bills and put the paid receipts back in that envelope, scratching out the words "to be." The envelope now reads "Bills Paid" for that month. You'll have an accurate, easy-to-find, complete record of all the bills you've paid each month, and between that and your checkbook and receipts, you'll have no trouble doing your income tax at the end of the year. Even more important, if three or four years hence the IRS wants some information from you, it will be on hand and easy to find.

INCOME TAX DEDUCTIBLE EXPENSES

Garden Equipment

tools	lumber
plants	fencing
seeds	fence posts
fertilizers	bricks
hoses and watering equipment	staple gun
carts	hand tools
harvest baskets	containers and buckets
soil	mulch

Office Expenses

typewriter	household electricity
calculator	gas or oil
desks and files	water and sewage
stationery and supplies	fix up supplies and labor

Special Items

hired hands' wages	accountant or lawyer fees
all car expenses related to delivery	garden magazines and books (including this one)
special boots and clothing	

If these items are purchased solely for your new business, keep receipts and they may be deducted as legitimate expenses on your income tax return.

To deduct auto expenses you can keep an accurate record backed by receipts of every dollar you spend for business travel in your family car. Or you can do it the easy way and just keep track of the approximate miles you drive. The IRS allows you to deduct so many cents per mile. That figure keeps changing although it's fixed by law for each year. It does take into consideration all costs of owning and maintaining a car, including gas and oil, repairs, tires and battery, and depreciation for wear and tear.

TRIP TICKET

Date _____

Trip to _____

Purpose _____

_____

Persons Visited _____

_____

Miles Driven _____

Gas/Oil _____

Parking _____

Meals _____

_____

_____

Telephone _____

Xerox _____

Other _____

_____

_____

_____

Total Expenses _____

Since all of your income and profit are in cash with no deductions for Social Security taxes, income taxes, or unemployment taxes that are usually taken out of your paycheck at the office or plant, you may have to file and pay what are called estimated payments four times a year with the IRS. It all depends on your expected income from your new cash garden business. Once you can reasonably estimate that, call your local IRS office and ask about this. You don't have to give your name, and you won't get in any trouble for asking, so don't be afraid to pick up the phone.

Property Tax Deduction

One item you might look into is a property tax deduction because of agricultural exemptions. Farmers in many states and countries have their land evaluated at a much lower rate than residential property, and it's possible that if you earned more than $300 or $500 or some amount established by your local tax department, you may be entitled to this exemption. This would result in your paying lower property taxes, another big advantage of having a cash business. In effect, if you can save money, it's the same as earning more income, and since you don't have to pay taxes on the amount saved, you're saving even more.

One question that always comes up is, "Should I remain a small business in the form of a sole proprietorship, or should I form a corporation?" You see lots of advertisements about how easy it is to form a corporation and all the advantages to it, but unless you're really into gardening on a large scale, you'll find it rather complicated. For example, although in many states you can form a corporation without hiring a lawyer, you'll find there are a lot of forms to fill out and reports to write, as well as a lot of rules and regulations to be aware of. You'll eventually have to hire a lawyer, and probably an accountant as well, to keep everything straight. You'll have to follow different tax laws, too. Instead of simply filling an additional page (Schedule C) on your income tax return, you'll have to fill out an entirely new report.

In the past, when I was finished with a business or wanted to end it, it cost more in lawyers' fees to dissolve the corporation than it did to incorporate in the first place. In fact, it took as long as five years to dissolve some businesses because of the horrendous state and federal regulations concerning corporations. My advice in most cases is to keep your business as small and simple as you can.

Information Available

If you feel the need for further information, the government has several free publications available on starting businesses. Send a postcard to:

U.S. Small Business Administration
Box 15434
Fort Worth, TX 76119

Ask for the pamphlet titled *Home Businesses* as well as the list of other free management assistance publications. These tell you much that is helpful about management, planning, administration, marketing, personnel, legal problems, and getting started. Most people find very little need for all this information for a small, simple business like cash gardening, but you may find it helpful.

In summary: the paperwork required for a small business may at first sound like a headache. But it isn't, unless you make it so.

Chapter 10

Garden Size, Location, and Layout

One of the advantages of square foot gardening is that it can be practiced profitably on relatively small spaces. A square foot garden takes only 20 percent of the space of a conventional garden. Even the quarter-acre lot of suburban homes is usually adequate.

That lot, about 11,000 square feet, is usually divided so that the house and garage take about 3,000 square feet, the driveway another 1,000, and the front and side yards 3,000. This leaves about 4,000 for the backyard. If you converted half of that (2,000 square feet) into a cash garden, you'll have room for almost 1,400 square feet of growing area while the remaining 600 square feet are in paths and non-productive areas. At an average yield of $5 per square foot, your cash garden could produce $7,000 a year for you.

Thus, the question you must answer is not about the space you have and need, but how much money you want to make, how much time you want to spend, and whether you can find a good market for your cash garden.

If your financial needs are modest, only part of your backyard may be needed for gardening; if you're very ambitious, you may want to use the entire backyard, even if you have more than 4,000 square feet, or you may even want to arrange for additional land.

The basic square foot system utilizes a four-foot square with a walking aisle on all four sides. Since the object of a cash garden is to have as much growing area as possible, you could give up a little convenience and arrange those squares end on end to form a long garden that's four feet wide. You'll have to walk around a long bed, but it will avoid a lot of non-productive space.

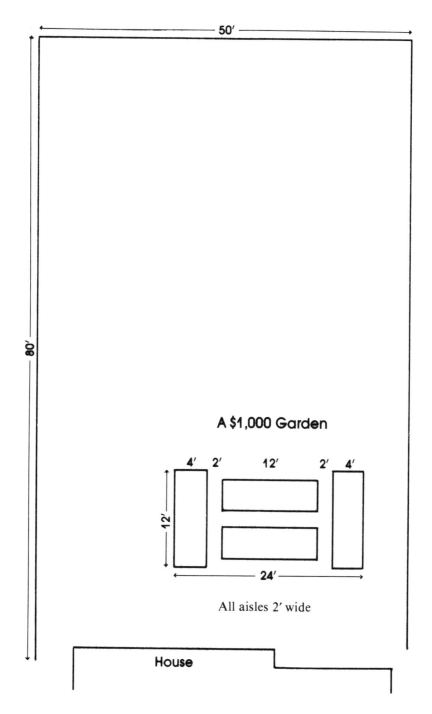

A $1,000 Garden

All aisles 2' wide

House

In this 50 X 80-foot backyard, these four beds will occupy 288 square feet, with 192 square feet used for growing. That's enough to produce an income of $960.

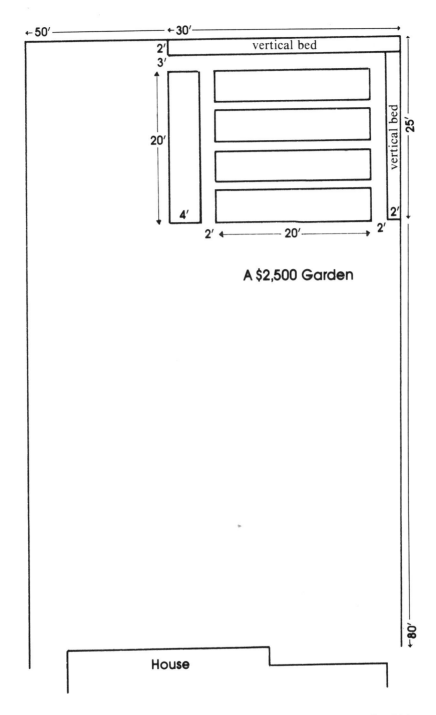

A $2,500 Garden

In the same backyard, these beds will take up 750 square feet, with 506 square feet used for growing. At $5 per square feet, this garden will yield $2,530.

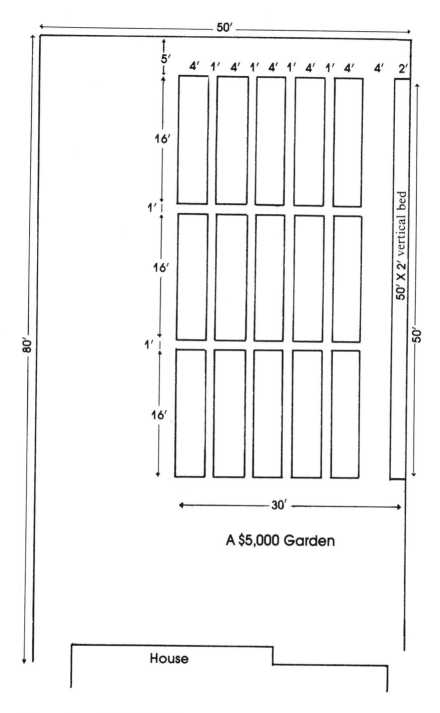

A $5,000 Garden

This garden will yield $5,320. The garden area is 1,500 square feet, of which 1,064 square feet is for growing areas.

Width of Aisles

The aisles can be as narrow as twelve inches, but most people feel more comfortable with aisles fifteen or eighteen inches wide. A rough layout of your yard and garden bed location will help you to decide on aisle width and bed length. In general, you'll use 60 to 70 percent of the garden area as productive growing areas.

Sun

If you have a small yard and nowhere else to garden, your choice of a site is limited. (On the other hand, it makes for a very easy decision.)

If you have a large yard, though, or you're considering gardening in some other location, your single most important consideration should be sun, sun, and more sun. Do not select a shaded area. You'll be continually fighting the sun/shade problem, and your production will be diminished. In fact, your site should not be even close to the shade of trees or shrubs, because they grow rapidly and soon will throw your garden into partial shade. The length of time you have full sun is most important. At least six to eight hours a day are needed for growing warm-weather or summer vegetables such as tomatoes, cucumbers, squash, peppers, and eggplant. Less is needed for cool-weather or spring crops of lettuce, beets, carrots, radishes, and onions. Four to six hours are enough.

Soil

Other considerations are not as important as sun. Take soil, for example. Unless you have several acres or your land slopes greatly, your soil will be fairly uniform throughout your property. Since the square foot system involves building up your soil in raised beds, you won't have to worry about your soil as you would in conventional gardening. This is explained in detail in chapter eleven.

Water

Another factor to consider is the availability of water. You won't want to lug water or run hoses a long distance, so pick a location that's close to a water spigot. If you have a large piece of property, and you're putting your garden way out back, seriously consider running a large (at least ¾-inch diameter), heavy-duty hose or buried pipe to the garden area.

Drainage

If your prospective site puddles for several hours after a heavy rain, it probably has poor drainage and may be a bad choice. If you must select a site where water flows onto it, there are several possible remedies, such as ditching and terracing, to divert the flow away from the garden. This is much easier than providing drainage within the area. Instead of starting off with a problem, though, try to pick an area that drains readily, and you'll be way ahead of the game.

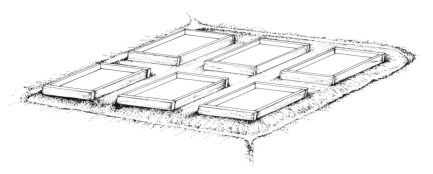

If drainage is a problem, dig a ditch around your garden area to carry water away from it.

Location

It's helpful to put your garden close to your house. You'll find it easier to care for the garden. Also, since you can see the garden from inside the house, it's easier to spot trouble such as munching rabbits.

You'll also find that the more often you look at the garden, the more often you'll go out to tend it. Since a square foot garden is so beautiful, every time you see it, you'll want to get out there for a closer look. With every short visit you will spot minor problems or a crop that's ready to be picked. Your garden will benefit from this added attention. In the long run, this will mean a larger cash harvest for you.

Security

If you can't put the garden close to the house, think about the security of the area you're selecting. Is it fenced in? Is it near a thoroughfare? Is it protected from neighborhood children? Is there much vandalism in your area? If your yard isn't already fenced, investing in a fence may be cost-effective in the long run.

Slope

If you have a lot of land, and have a choice of slope—that is, if part of the land slopes to the south and another part slopes to the north—garden the slope that points towards the sun. That spot will be the warmest and it will warm up earlier in the spring. You'll be able to plant sooner, and to a cash gardener that means more money. Most people don't have this choice, but if you're one of the lucky few, make the best use of this advantage.

When deciding where to put your garden, look over your entire property. There may be areas that you might have overlooked during the first go-around, as well as areas that could be used if your garden were split up. Many people turn their side yard or even their front yard into a cash garden. A square foot garden certainly is attractive and would enhance any yard, regardless of its location.

Other Land

If you have a small yard and don't want to use it for gardening, there's no reason why you have to use your backyard. Why not someone else's? Some friendly neighbor who always wanted an attractive garden, or who might want to earn some extra money by renting you a piece—or even all—of his backyard? This is a particularly welcome solution if you live in a heavily wooded area that gets very little sun, or if your landscaping doesn't adapt well to a large garden. You can also rent empty lots or side lots. Or you may be able to find someone who already has a large garden and wouldn't mind having you as a friendly tenant.

You might not even have to pay rent if you go about it the right way. Companionship and common interests are both persuasive reasons. You might also be able to barter or trade some of your services for use of that land. Why not help take care of the yard? Or supply that family with all the vegetables they can eat, harvested fresh from your garden?

Accessibility

One last thing to keep in mind is accessibility to your vehicle. You have to pull up to load your harvest a couple of times a week, and you won't want to lug it very far. In addition, since you'll be building some wooden frames and bringing in a lot of soil, manure, and other supplies, your garden should be fairly close to the driveway or an area where a truck can easily back up.

Laying Out the Garden

Once you've selected a garden site, the next step is to lay it out. Using the square foot system, you'll be dividing it into blocks four feet square or into long beds that are four feet wide. You must decide what direction they'll run and how wide the aisles between them should be.

In general, keep your vertical frames on the north side, and when planting, keep the taller plants on the north side.

Lay out the beds in your garden in any pattern you find attractive and convenient to work around.

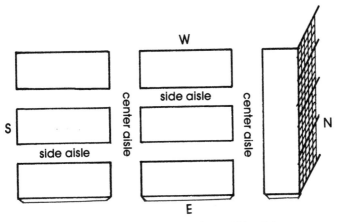

A 3- or 4-foot center aisle is convenient. Side aisles can be from 12 to 18 inches in width. Locate vertical beds on the north side of your garden.

Wide Aisle

It's usually most efficient to lay out a center aisle wide enough for a cart or even an automobile. This will be used for harvesting, washing, and removing your produce. The side aisles should be only wide enough for walking and kneeling. Remember, your objective is to have as much growing area as possible. Because you can reach in at least two feet from each side, your growing areas can be four feet wide instead of the conventional square foot gardening system of four-foot squares bordered on all four sides by walking paths. Depending on the existing surface, and how you want your garden to look, you might leave grass growing in the aisles (just make sure they're wide enough to run a lawn mower through), cover them with planks, or lay down carpeting or other mulching material to prevent weeds from growing. All of these materials will keep your feet dry and your clothes clean while you're working in the garden.

Building Borders

Your beds should be bordered with wood if possible. This makes for a neater garden which is easier to take care of, and it allows you to build up your soil more easily and to cover individual beds more readily for protection (see chapter three). The ideal size for lumber is two-by-sixes or two-by-eights. This is fairly expensive if you buy it, but you should be able to find some for free. There's always some construction in the neighborhood and builders throw away a lot of good lumber. Just ask the foreman. Chances are he's a gardener and will have a personal interest in your project. Some inquisitive builders have even offered to deliver the lumber so they could look at my garden plan. Be careful: you don't want to tell too much about your new business or you may have an unemployed builder as your new competitor.

MATERIALS FOR AISLES

Wooden planks	Neat and clean, expensive if bought new; lift to catch slugs.
Plywood strips	Neat and clean, expensive if bought new; lift to catch slugs.
Black plastic	Cheap but unattractive, unless covered with mulch; punch holes for drainage.
Bricks	Expensive but attractive; not soft for kneeling.
Crushed stone	Expensive but attractive; drain well, but not comfortable.
Grass	Attractive, needs mowing and edging.
Cardboard	Cheap but unattractive unless covered with hay or leaves.
Outdoor carpet	A good idea. Often can be obtained used for free at a rug store.
Mulch materials	Hay, dried grass, leaves. All attractive and free or inexpensive.
Plain old dirt	Use action hose weekly for easy weeding.

Building Frames

Construct your wood frames by nailing four boards together, four feet long at each end and as long at the sides as you want each bed to be. If you don't have lumber that's long enough for the sides (let's say twelve feet long), you can easily splice two pieces together. Butt the ends together and put a piece of plywood on the inside, nail

It's easiest to assemble the wood border on a hard, flat surface like a driveway.

it through, and hammer the nails flat. This creates a fairly strong joint that is still slim and won't get in the way when you're turning your soil or planting.

With these joints you can construct beds that are the length you want. Firm up the soil around the wood. It won't have to withstand much pressure, so don't worry too much about driving in stakes or providing other supports, as many books recommend when building bordered bed gardens.

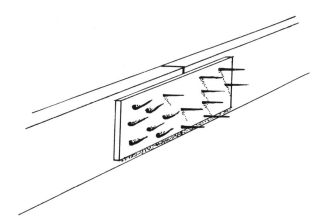

To splice lumber, use a small piece of plywood, nailed on the inside of the bed, and bend over the nail ends.

If you're not going to rototill, nail spacers of two-by-fours or two-by-sixes across every four feet. This should be the only support your frames will need; it also provides built-in visual guidance for spacing your plants. Then it's easy to plant one, two, or four linear feet of your bed area each week with a different crop.

Build Up Beds

Next, strip the weeds or grass from the beds, loosen the existing soil, and fill your frames with the best soil mixture you can afford. (See chapter eleven for more details.) With few exceptions, your existing soil will not be good enough to grow an optimum cash garden. If you can't afford to buy bags of prepared soil mix (the ideal solution), it's better to fill your frames gradually with as much compost, manure, peat moss, and vermiculite as you can. They don't have to be filled to the brim immediately. If you're in a rush and fill your frames with poor growing soil, you'll be stuck with it forever. It's very unlikely that you'll ever replace it. If you bring in good things gradually, you'll be surprised at how quickly your frames will fill up.

In laying out your garden area, your final decisions will concern the number of beds and what you're going to grow. Will it be short, medium, or tall, and will you have frames for your vertical crops? You should plan to put your tall plants on vertical frames, to the north side so they won't shade the shorter plants. Group vulnerable crops together if you have pest problems. For example, if rabbits or deer are common in your neighborhood, group lettuce, spinach, and peas so they can be more easily protected with fencing. Radishes, carrots, and onions could go in a different area, since rabbits and deer are not as fond of them.

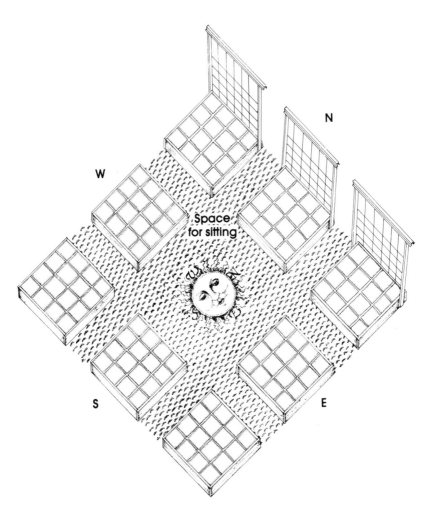

A garden of squares and aisles can be both practical and attractive.

To anyone choosing the ultimate size of a garden, my advice is the same as it is to beginning square foot gardeners: start small; you can always expand. You'll be much more successful if you stay small at the beginning, take good care of what you have, and learn to handle that before moving on to a larger enterprise.

Chapter 11
Soil Preparation

 Whether you garden organically or non-organically, you must have the best possible soil, soil that will produce bumper crops.

Since most soil is far from good, you must build up a rich, humusy, well-drained soil. In conventional gardens, this might be prohibitively expensive. But that's not true in square foot gardening, since it requires only 20 percent of the space of a conventional garden for an equal amount of produce.

First step in preparing a bed is to strip off the grass, then loosen the subsoil, removing rocks and roots.

I have two recommendations.

1. Right at the beginning, build perfect soil.

2. Start small and prepare the perfect soil for the size garden that you can afford.

Don't start out by planting a large garden in poor soil. You'll only be wasting your time and producing a poor harvest.

Organic?

Decide now whether you're going to grow organically or non-organically. This is a matter of personal choice. Organically grown produce often commands a much higher price; however, it's much harder to grow a crop without pest damage. You might find that in some areas of the country, there is little demand for organically grown produce. It therefore brings a much lower price if it has a less than perfect look. Some non-organic gardeners later find a more profitable market for organically grown, so they switch. But I wouldn't let the market decide how you're going to grow. I'd say that depends on how you feel about it. To be truly organic, you should not have used any chemicals, chemical fertilizers, or insecticides in that soil for at least the past couple of years.

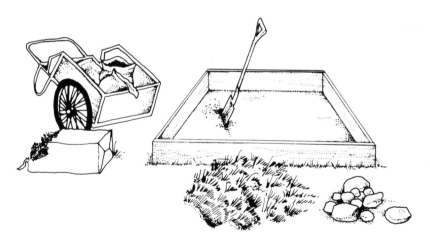

After stripping the sod and removing rocks and roots, mix in a 3-inch layer of perfect soil mix, then fill the box with this same mix. Level it and you're ready to start planting.

Whether you grow organically or non-organically, your perfect soil must be rich, humusy, well-drained, and friable. The basic ingredients are always the same: peat moss, vermiculite, and compost. If you want to take the quick and easy route, you'll buy large bags of prepared soil mix. That's what the commercial greenhouse growers do. There are few, if any, large commercial growers today who mix their own soil. They all buy it in bags or bales. Because it's composed mostly of vermiculite and peat moss, it contains nothing that could contaminate an organic garden. It can be purchased at nursery supply centers. They're listed in the phone book. Contact your local nursery; tell them you need a certain number of large (try to get the four cubic feet) bags or bales.

How to Estimate

Here's how to estimate how many you'll need. Each four-by-four planting area equals sixteen square feet. If the new soil is one foot deep, you'll need sixteen times one or sixteen cubic feet. If it is only half that deep, or six inches deep, you would need half of the sixteen or eight cubic feet.

The mixes are compressed into bales of either four, five, or six cubic feet. Every manufacturer packs his mixture slightly differently from others, and they don't tell you on the bag how much the loose volume is. They just state the compressed volume. Figure it will double in volume.

So, add up your total bed areas, then decide the depth you need of new planting mix. If the existing soil is poor, remove it. If it is halfway decent, it can be mixed with the planting mix. Also consider the amount of compost or well-rotted manure you can get to mix in. Then you can estimate a little closer the number of bales you'll need.

Don't be too concerned about the exact amount. It's not critical if your beds aren't up to the top with new planting mix. You can keep adding compost and manure as the months and years go by. Every time you replant an area, you'll add compost to it. That will bring the level up another half-inch to an inch.

Loose Mixes

If you buy bags of loose mix, you're going to get exactly the amount stated on the bag. Sometimes vermiculite is sold in six-cubic-foot as well as four-cubic-foot bags. Again, it depends on the manufacturer, what part of the country you're in, and your source. Take an example: your beds are twelve feet long by four feet wide, and your existing soil is halfway decent. You decide to add three inches of planting mix. The quantity you need would be twelve times four, times three inches over twelve inches (or one-fourth of a foot). That equals twelve cubic feet.

If you buy four-cubic-foot bales of compressed planting mix, you'll need one and a half bales for each bed. That's six cubic feet of compressed mix, which will expand to double, or the twelve cubic feet you need.

SOIL VOLUME

This table shows the amount of soil required to fill a 4X4 area at various depths.

Depth	Number of Cubic Feet
12″	16
8″	11
6″	8
4″	5½
3″	4
2″	2½
(1 bushel basket = 1.24 cubic feet.)	

Quality Varies

The quality of planting mixes varies. There are many companies in the business. Some are regional and others are national. And their products differ. Some materials are rather fine, some are fairly coarse. As you can expect, the less expensive ones have more coarse material. Sometimes you'll find a lot of sticks and stones in the mix, because it was not screened very well. Look over the mixes before you decide which to buy. The nursery or the garden supply center you're buying from should be able to help you with this. You also might want to talk with local growers. They could advise you as to which brand they like the best. Remember, they're using it for different purposes, for starting seeds in flats or potting houseplants or flowers. Because you're gardening outdoors and raising primarily vegetables, you might want a coarser mix that won't pack down with the rain and normal use, if you have a clay soil. You might also want to mix in some sand, which is very inexpensive, before adding the new soil mix on top. The sand will help to break up the clay, and stretch your expensive planting mix a little further. Of course, if you have a very sandy soil, you don't want to add more sand to it.

One note of caution to organic gardeners: sometimes the planting mixes that you buy in commercial bags contain a small amount of chemical starter fertilizer. Check the labels to make sure the mix doesn't contain this fertilizer.

Mix Your Own

As an alternative to the ready mix, you can purchase individual bags of vermiculite and peat moss to mix your own. They both come in bags or bales containing four or six cubic feet. When buying vermiculite, get the coarse grade, rather than the fine or medium. Since it gradually breaks down, you want to start with the largest particles you can. Vermiculite is mica rock that has been heated until it expands, just like popcorn.

The type of peat moss is not particularly important. Most growers use either peat or sphagnum, domestic or imported. They believe the qualities are about the same. Some will argue that point, but it usually boils down to a matter of personal choice.

Need for Compost

There is one thing that commercial growers don't have, but you should have, and that is compost. If you don't have any, you may be able to find it nearby. Many communities collect leaves in the fall and compost them, offering the decomposed material free to community residents.

Since compost is nothing but leaves and other vegetable matter that have decomposed, you might scout around your neighborhood. Try the town dump or an area where the town sweepers deposit their loads. Local farms may have piles of manure or hay that has decomposed. These are fine for your compost ingredient.

The easiest place to get raw materials for your compost pile is at grocery stores. They throw out crate after crate of spoiled cabbage and lettuce, beet tops, carrot tops, and all types of greens. A friendly visit with the produce manager will assure you of a continual supply. Because it's green and moist, it will start decaying rapidly in your compost pile. Don't put it directly into your garden.

If you have dried leaves to mix with all this fresh, green material, all the better. If not, you might try shredded newspapers. Make sure you use only the black and white pages; color pages do not decompose readily and contain some harmful materials. And, of course, if you don't have a compost pile, get one started immediately.

You can start your garden by building your beds on top of the existing soil. If it's really poor, you can remove some of it and use it for your paths. Even though you'll have to buy more of the soil mix, you'll be better off in the long run, especially if your existing soil doesn't drain well.

Testing the Soil

Everyone wants to know when to add fertilizer, and how much. But there's another step that's more important. You should check the acidity of your soil by measuring the pH. This can be done by taking a sample to your local nursery or county agricultural agent, or by testing it yourself with an inexpensive pH test kit. You'll want a pH level between 6 and 7. Anything below that indicates a very acid soil which will need additional lime. A pH above 7 indicates a very alkaline soil which will need additional sulfur. The amount you add depends on the levels of your present soil on the pH scale. Follow the directions on the lime or sulfur package label.

Many gardening books describe how some crops prefer soil of a very specific pH. Except for extremely acid-loving crops such as blueberries, you don't have to worry about pH preference. Most crops will do well in the range between 6 and 7. Some will tolerate a lower pH and some a higher, but what's overlooked by most garden books is that most crops will do well within the 6-7 range.

Fertilizers

Now we're ready to discuss fertilizers—how much to add, when, and what type. When you go shopping, you'll see a bewildering array of formulas on the shelves. Most mixes are labeled "complete" or "balanced," meaning they contain a certain percentage of the three main ingredients, nitrogen, phosphorus, and potassium, and small amounts of the important trace elements.

The percentages are designated by hyphenated numbers, such as 5-10-5 or 5-10-10. To complicate matters, they come in powdered, granular, and water-soluble forms. What to use?

I usually use about ten pounds of fertilizer per 100 square feet of garden area, or one pound per ten square feet. That's a little more than half a one-pound coffee can added to each four-by-four planting area. Mix it in well with the soil.

The formula you buy should be a very basic one, and the cheapest is usually a 5-10-5 or a 5-10-10 formula. The first number represents the nitrogen, and that's the most expensive ingredient. When you're beginning your basic soil preparation, you don't want to add too much nitrogen. It either disintegrates quickly in an inactive soil or is used up rapidly by developing plants. The other two ingredients,

FERTILIZER APPLICATION

N Nitrogen *For leaf crops*	P Phosphorus *For fruit crops*	K Potassium *For root crops*
Lettuce	Tomatoes	Radishes
Spinach	Peppers	Carrots
Cabbage	Beans	Turnips

Initial soil preparation:

- Use granular 5-10-5 or similar strength
- 1 pound per 10 square feet
- 1½ pounds per four-foot garden square

Periodic Application:

- Plants growing less than six weeks, no extra applications.
- Plants growing more than six weeks, use granular or water-soluble at half-strength every two weeks. Follow directions on label.
- Plants that have blossoms, apply an extra feeding of half-strength high-phosphorus formula every other week during blossoming.

phosphorus and potassium, last longer. Later on, you'll probably find it more convenient to use a water-soluble fertilizer so you don't disturb the soil around your plants. But I always use a basic 5-10-5 granular fertilizer whenever I prepare the soil for a new planting.

Stripping Soil

Once your beds and walking paths are laid out, remove any sod or weeds growing in your planting areas. This sod probably contains the best growing soil you have in your backyard, so don't throw it away. It can be added to your compost pile but should be turned upside down to make the sod decay faster. It could also be transplanted to your paths to cover any bare spots, if you want grass growing in your paths. But it should *not* be turned upside down and spaded into your growing area. Grass has a way of continuing to grow long after you think it should be dead.

Tilling the Soil

One question that always comes up is, "Should I rototill my garden, or should I try hand digging with a pickaxe, shovel, or fork?"

It depends on how deep you want to go, how thoroughly you want to break up the soil, and how often you expect to turn the soil. These features, in turn, are determined by how good your soil is. Remember: in the square foot gardening system, you do not walk on your growing soil. It won't get packed down and won't require continual digging and turning over as it does in most garden systems. I recommend that people dig only as deep as their backs allow. You don't want to injure yourself because you've assumed that the deeper you dig, the better your plants will grow. Contrary to what we've read, the roots of most vegetables remain fairly shallow. This is especially true in a square foot garden, where you provide the perfect soil, maintain ideal watering conditions, and eliminate competition from weeds. Your plants won't have to send roots down several feet looking for moisture or nutrients, as so many conventional gardening books have stated. Deep digging is not as important in the square foot garden.

If you plan to rototill, be very careful. Although rototillers look as if they're doing a wonderful job, they don't go very deep. If you want to mix your existing soil with your new soil, do it in layers.

The first step: pour in and rake out about a three-inch layer of new planting mix. Either dig or rototill that, mixing it in with the existing soil. If you're rototilling, you're not going to go very deep, but you will mix the two soils. If you're hand digging, take your time, and go as deep as you're comfortable digging. If you have a strong high school boy working for you, tell him to go down the depth of the shovel blade.

Turn the soil over, break up clods, and mix the good with the existing soil. Rake that out level, removing sticks, roots, any man-made debris, and certainly any large stones.

Next, pour in another layer of three or four inches of the good planting mix and mix that with the existing mixed soil. Rake that level, and add, as a final topping, two or three inches more of the good planting mix. You now have a pretty good soil that gradually goes from a perfect planting mix at the top to a predominantly good mix at the next step, to a fifty-fifty mix at the bottom. Below that you have your existing soil.

As you add new compost and manure through the months and years, you'll be turning in this material, but since it's now soft, loose, and friable, you won't have much work to do.

The first step is a lot of work and physically exhausting, so take your time. If you're doing it yourself, by hand, do one small area at a time, perhaps just a four-by-four-foot area, and then take a break. Come back to your beds later in the day, or perhaps the next day. Everything does not have to be done at once.

Your result will be a very nice soil mix that will last for many years and provide you with the ideal medium for your cash garden, regardless of what your existing soil was.

Rototilling

Those who use a rototiller will find that everything should go very easily, but they must go back over the area a few times. Don't add the full depth of your new planting mix and think that you're going to mix that into your existing soil. The rototiller will just not go that deep, regardless of what brand you have. You must do it in layers. Although a rototiller is a great labor-saving device, because it will not go deep enough, I find hand digging is much more satisfactory.

Of course, if you have a very heavy clay soil—one of those Louisiana gumbos or California clays—it is extremely hard to dig and mix it well. This is where a rototiller is most useful, because it can mix and break up your existing soils. You'll probably end up with a better job of mixing in the new material.

Layering Materials

Whether you're digging or rototilling, you should add fertilizer and pH adjustment material, either lime or sulfur, as you add each layer. It's probably most important to do that bottom layer, because your existing soil requires the most amendments. Divide the total amount in half or thirds, depending on how many layers you're going to do. Again, it's not critical. It's an estimation you make merely by eye and feel. As you do each layer, begin by sprinkling over the surface the fertilizer and lime or sulfur. As that gets mixed in, and you add your next layer of new material, add another sprinkling of fertilizer and lime or sulfur.

The prepared soil mixes are fairly close to the ideal pH level. Some of them run a little acid, with a pH of 5 to 6, so you'll want to add a little bit of lime to them. None of the prepared soil mixes is alkaline, so you don't have to worry about adding sulfur. In the western states, where there's little rainfall, the natural soil may be above 7, and will require sulfur. In other states, where there's a fairly heavy rainfall, over twenty or thirty inches a year, the natural soil is anywhere from neutral to slightly acid, down to a very acid soil in the heavy rainfall areas.

Supports Needed

A problem you may have with this soil is that, because it's so loose and friable, heavier plants may fall over in heavy winds or rain. I'll show you how to build simple, inexpensive supports in chapter fourteen.

The final step is to rake the soil level, then to decide what method of planting you will use.

The hill-and-furrow method is ideal for closely spaced plants, hot, dry climates, and areas of the country that limit the use of water for gardens. It is also ideal for plants that require uniform moisture. To plant using this method, you shape the bed into a series of furrows, spaced so that seeds can be planted at the proper distance apart and in the bottom of each furrow. Thus, when the bed is watered, the moisture runs to the bottom of the furrow where it is most needed.

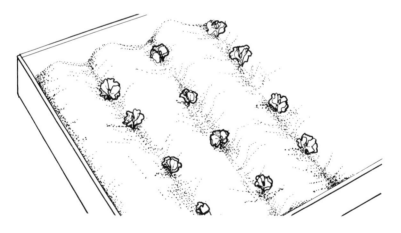

In arid areas, shape your soil into hills, then plant on the lower levels. Plant lettuce 6 inches apart, beans, 4 inches, and carrots, 3 inches.

Plant lettuce in dish-shaped depressions, for easier watering later.

Cup-and-saucer planting is best for widely spaced plants such as peppers and eggplants, which won't be injured if the saucer fills in during a heavy rainstorm.

Cup-and-saucer planting is placing each plant in a saucer-shaped depression about the width of the full-grown plant and about one inch deep. By watering in these saucers, you ensure that the moisture goes down to the roots, and that you're not watering where you will encourage the growth of weeds.

For those who want the ultimate in water conservation, try my New York Times garden (sometimes called the Chicago Tribune garden). It combines the hill and furrow shape with a mulch of newspapers. First, shape the soil to the spacing of whatever you're planting. Then lay down a six-page thickness of newspaper to cover the hills. You can leave a one-inch strip of soil showing at the bottom of the furrow if you're planting seeds. If you're putting in transplants, you might cover all the soil with newspaper and then poke a hole in the paper for each plant, using a knife.

No weeds can grow through the paper, and all water rolls down the hill and into the furrow.

Soil preparation is going to be not only the most expensive part of your garden, but the most work as well. Don't skimp on this step because it is the entire foundation of your business. Without good growing soil, you will constantly struggle to produce a decent crop.

You should hear the comments of gardeners who have switched to the square foot method and have taken the time, trouble, and expense to obtain the perfect soil. They say it's like a whole new world of gardening. It really makes that much difference.

So start small and build only as many boxes as you can fill with a perfect soil mix. Don't be tempted to fill them with a load of topsoil or bags of $1.29 black soil on sale, or even the soil in your garden. Stick with the perfect soil mix and enjoy gardening like you never have before.

Chapter 12
Scheduling Your Crops

$ Well, you've selected your market and made all the arrangements with your prospective buyers; you've laid out your garden and prepared your soil. Now it's time to get down to the final preparation, deciding what crops you plan to grow. Ask yourself these questions. Are you sure you can sell these crops? Are they in demand? Are they fairly easy to grow? Will they realize a good profit for the space and time required?

By starting with crops that are easy to grow, you will help guarantee your success. Give yourself every advantage possible this first year and save the challenging crops for later. Some people feel the need to tell their friends and neighbors they're growing exotic or difficult crops such as artichokes or mangoes; some might even be embarrassed to say they're selling radishes out of their backyards. Don't be a show-off. Just say you're growing salad crops for a local restaurant, and your vanity will be soothed when you look at your bank balance.

What Amounts?

In addition to listing those crops you plan to grow, start thinking about the amounts that you're going to need—how many radishes or heads of leaf lettuce per week. You should have discussed this with your buyer and he should have given you some indication of how much he uses each week. Supplying him with 20 or 30 percent of that amount should be your goal. Since it's so much easier to produce a perfect crop in a square foot garden than in a single row garden, you don't have to resort to the farmers' technique of overplanting in order to produce a reasonable harvest. If all goes well,

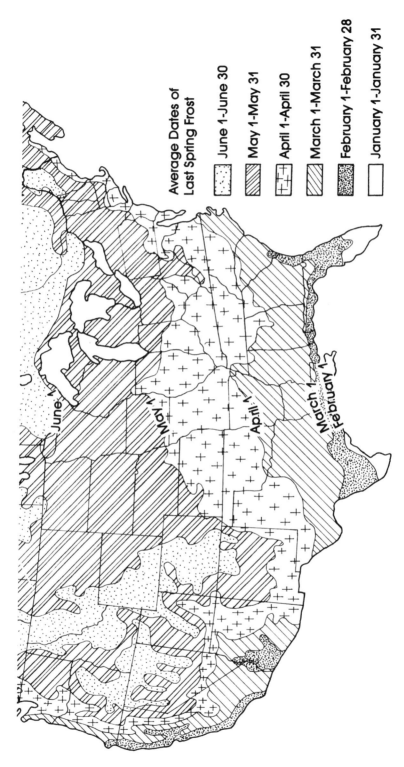

Average Dates of
Last Spring Frost

June 1-June 30

May 1-May 31

April 1-April 30

March 1-March 31

February 1-February 28

January 1-January 31

June 1

May 1

April 1

March 1

February 1

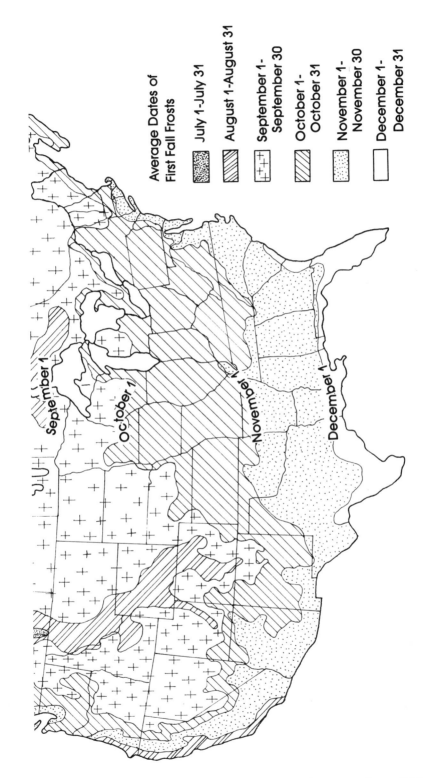

Average Dates of
First Fall Frosts

July 1-July 31

August 1-August 31

September 1-
September 30

October 1-
October 31

November 1-
November 30

December 1-
December 31

September 1

October 1

November 1

December 1

you should be able to harvest and sell 80 to 90 percent of everything planted. But you must be able to provide a continuous supply. Once you stop delivering a certain item on a regular basis, your buyer will turn to other sources. Don't go four weeks without delivering carrots, then suddenly show up with a large harvest. Also, tell your buyer in advance when a particular supply will be exhausted, so that he can find a source to replace it.

ESTIMATING YOUR PROFITS

We interviewed the owner of a small (forty-five seats) restaurant who said he could use the following salad vegetables *every week* and was willing, even eager, to buy as many as possible from us. We've figured on the basis of furnishing 30 percent of his needs.

Crop	100%	30%	# Per Sq. Ft.	Area Needed in Sq. Ft.
Radishes	9 pounds=400 each	120 ÷	16 =	8
Carrots	25 pounds=250 each	75 ÷	16 =	5
Leaf lettuce	24 heads=24 heads	7 ÷	4 =	2
Romaine let.	24 heads=24 heads	7 ÷	4 =	2
Scallions	20 bunches=120 each	36 ÷	25 =	1½

If you were to supply 30 percent of his needs, you would need the following space.

Radishes: Need 4 weeks growing
                          X 8 square feet per week
                          _____
                          = 32 square feet of garden space.
Plant 8 square feet every week.

Carrots: Need 12 weeks growing
                         X 5 square feet per week
                         _____
                         = 60 square feet of garden space.
Plant 5 square feet every week.

Leaf lettuce: Need 5 weeks growing
                              X 2 square feet per week
                              _____
                              = 10 square feet of garden space.
Plant 2 square feet every week.

Romaine lettuce: Same as leaf lettuce.

Scallions: Need 6 weeks growing
$$\underline{\text{X } 1\tfrac{1}{2} \text{ square feet per week}}$$
= 9 square feet of garden space.

Plant 1½ square feet every week.

TOTAL Garden space:

Radishes	32 square feet
Carrots	60
Leaf lettuce	10
Romaine lettuce	10
Scallions	9

TOTAL   121 square feet

Two beds, 4 feet wide X 15 feet long = 120 square feet.

SALES

Radishes	120 X 5¢ = $ 6.00
Carrots	75 X 12¢ = 9.00
Leaf lettuce	7 X 79¢ = 5.50
Romaine lettuce	7 X 79¢ = 5.50
Scallions	36 X 7¢ = 2.50

TOTAL		
	$ 28.50	per week
	X 4	
	$115.00	per month
	X 6	
	$690.00	per season

YIELD:

$$\frac{690}{120 \text{ square feet}} = \$5.75 \text{ per square foot}$$

I know a lot of people who would be tickled pink to earn almost $30 a week for working a few hours a week in such a small garden.

Of course you could double your area and supply the restaurant with 60 percent of its needs and earn almost $1,500, but remember that if you try to supply almost all of the needs of a restaurant, your problems will multiply. It would be better, if you want to raise a larger garden, to find a bigger restaurant.

Your buyer may be interested in having a seasonal item such as kale, which is available only in the fall. He may even be willing to plan his menu around such an item, but you must let him know well ahead of time what will be ready. Keep him aware of what you have now, what you'll have in the following weeks, and what you anticipate in the future. Otherwise you may end up with a harvest no one is interested in, and how much is that worth?

Keep Planting

In order to ensure the success of your business, you must keep planting, growing, and harvesting. And you must do it on schedule, so there's always something coming along. The worst thing you can do is deviate from your delivery schedule, or show up every week with apologies about being out of this or short on that. Your customer is bound to become disgruntled with your services. Of course, it's hard at first to figure out exactly how long it will take from planting seeds to delivering the harvest, but I'll explain how to set up charts that will help you plant on a schedule. Then you can make slight adjustments depending on the weather.

Cold Weather Crops		Warm Weather Crops	
Frost-Hardy Planted spring and again in fall; In southern and western coastal states, can be planted all winter.		Tender Planted summer only; In southern and western coastal states, can be grown in spring and fall.	
Beets	Swiss chard	Beans	Peppers
Broccoli	Onions	Cantaloupe	Squash,
Cabbage	Peas	Corn	summer
Carrots	Radishes	Cucumbers	and winter
Cauliflower	Spinach	Eggplant	Tomatoes

You must know the hardy crops, which can be planted in early, mid-, and late spring; the tender crops that must wait until summer; and those that can be planted in late summer for harvesting in the fall. Depending on your area of the country, estimate the length of your growing season and decide how far into the cold weather you'd like to (and can) garden.

Prepare a Calendar

I find it very helpful to cut up a calendar and piece it together so that the months form a planning chart that can be seen at a glance. Use one of those free bank calendars. Indicate your frost dates for spring and fall; then you can establish when to plant your seeds and transplants (both indoors and outdoors) in relation to these two dates. This all sounds like a lot of work, but it's really not. In fact it's almost as much fun as looking through the seed catalogs in mid-winter and deciding which seeds to buy for the coming year.

If you consult the charts on continuous harvest, you'll be able to plan how often you should replant the various crops. If you rely solely on watching the growth of your plants, you're going to get fooled. Seeds take a long time to sprout, and the seedlings seem so small that there's a tendency to wait until the plants become a "decent size" before you put in another crop. But keep in mind that you want to deliver this crop weekly, so you must plant weekly. Of course if it's one of the continuous-harvest crops such as tomatoes, cucumbers, or peppers, you should consider an early-, mid-, and late-season crop. All these plants have a peak period of harvest, and if you put everything in at once, you'll be overwhelmed during the few weeks of that harvest. To avoid this, you should stagger your plantings by a few weeks, or you can spread out your harvest by planting early, mid-season, and late varieties all at the same time.

Set up a complete schedule for seed starting and transplanting indoors, growing time for seedlings, setting outside or transplanting into the garden, growth to maturity, and expected dates for harvesting. Naturally, your crops will vary a bit from this schedule depending on growing conditions, but this will give you a rough idea of when you can replant each space with a new crop.

To determine when it's safe to start, look up your area on the frost maps to find your average last spring frost and first fall frost. Mark those dates on your strip calendar. The time between those two dates is your frost-free growing season.

Keep in mind that the frost charts are only approximate, based on averages calculated over many years. In fact, the criticism has recently been made that these charts are based on data that are extremely outdated, and that many do not include the last twenty to thirty years of weather data. Although updating probably wouldn't change them very much, keep in mind that your actual dates are going to vary by one or two weeks in either direction.

STRIP CALENDAR FOR PLANTING DATES

S	M	T	W	T	F	S
			1	2	3	4
5	6	7	8	9	10	11
12	13	14	15	16	17	18
19	20	21	22	23	24	25
26	27	28	29	30	31	1
2	3	4	5	6	7	8
9	10	11	12	13	14 Lettuce	15
16	17	18	19	20	21	22
23	24	25	26	27	28	1
2	3	4	5	6	7	8
9	10	11	12	13	14 Lettuce	15
16	17	18	19	20	21	22
23	24	25	26	27	28	29
30	31	1	2	3	4	5
6	7	8	9	10 Frost Free Date	11 Lettuce	12
13	14	15	16	17	18	19

Left margin (top to bottom): JANUARY, FEBRUARY, MARCH, APRIL

Right margin: Start lettuce seeds indoors — 4 weeks — Lettuce transplants go outdoors — 4 weeks — Harvest lettuce

Key

- Start seeds indoors
- Plant seeds outdoors
- Transplants go outdoors
- Harvest

Ready to Gamble

How early you start planting outdoors depends on how much of a gambler you are. Do you like to play it safe or do you prefer to take chances? If you're a middle-of-the-road type, gamble by putting part of your crop out early, but saving most of it for a safe planting date. This complicates your schedule a little, though, and probably should be saved for next year when you'll be more experienced at the whole business. Remember again, you want to play it safe and give yourself as many advantages as you can the first year, so why not select safe planting dates just to make sure you don't get wiped out by a late spring frost?

The other consideration is how well you are prepared to protect your garden. If your covers are ready, if there are enough to go around, they all fit properly, and are in good repair, and if you know how to use them, it's an easy matter to throw on some protection from an impending hailstorm or late frost. This will make your gamble less risky by evening up your odds against Mother Nature.

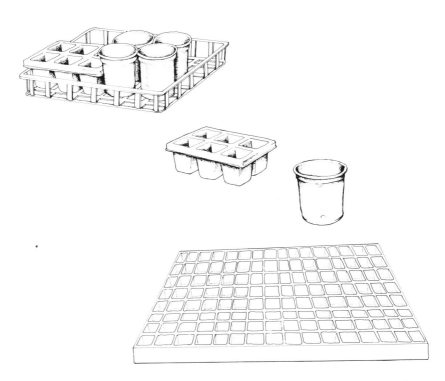

A variety of containers can be used for transplants and for starting seeds.

When to Start

The next schedules show when it's safe to plant outdoors as well as when to start seeds indoors. If you are growing your own transplants, the schedules also show how often you should replant in order to have a continuous harvest for sale.

In general, if you're growing something that's harvested by pulling up the entire plant, such as lettuce, radishes, and scallions, you should replant every week. If it's a crop like beans or peas that has a continuous harvest over three or four weeks, you should replant every two weeks so there is a little overlap in harvests. For those vegetables that have a harvest all season, such as tomatoes, cucumbers, and Swiss chard, you only have to plant once, unless you want a staggered harvest. Then you might plant one-third of your crop as early as possible, the next third two weeks later, and the final third in two more weeks.

You may want to make a similar schedule for your frost dates and just those crops you're going to grow. See if your area requires some adjustment in growing times or length of harvest. By combining these schedules with your strip calendar, you should have a fairly simple yet complete time schedule for your activities of the year.

A pencil is handy for quick and easy potting of seedlings.

EARLIEST PLANTING DATES

Your Last Spring Frost Date _____
(Safe Date)

	Start Seeds Indoors		Plant Transplants Outdoors	
	# of Weeks Before Safe Date	Your Actual Date	# of Weeks Before Safe Date	Your Actual Date
Broccoli	12	_____	5	_____
(Repeat Planting in 2 Weeks)		_____	2	_____
Cabbage	12	_____	5	_____
(Repeat Planting in 2 Weeks)		_____	2	_____
Cauliflower	10	_____	4	_____
(Repeat Planting in 2 Weeks)		_____	2	_____
Eggplant	7	_____	2	_____
Lettuce	7	_____	4	_____
(Repeat Planting Every Week)		_____	Every Week	_____
Peppers	7	_____	2	_____
Spinach	7	_____	4	_____
(Repeat Planting) Every Week		_____	Every Week	_____
Tomatoes	6	_____	On Safe Date	_____

Start Seeds Outdoors

	# of Weeks Before Safe Date	Your Actual Date
Beans (bush)	On Safe Date	_____
(Repeat Planting Every 2 Weeks)		_____
Beans (pole)	On Safe Date	_____
Carrots	3	_____
(Repeat Planting Every 2 Weeks)		_____
Beets	3	_____
(Repeat Planting Every 2 Weeks)		_____
Peas	5	_____
Radishes	3	_____
(Repeat Planting Every Week)		_____

SPRING INDOOR SEED STARTING

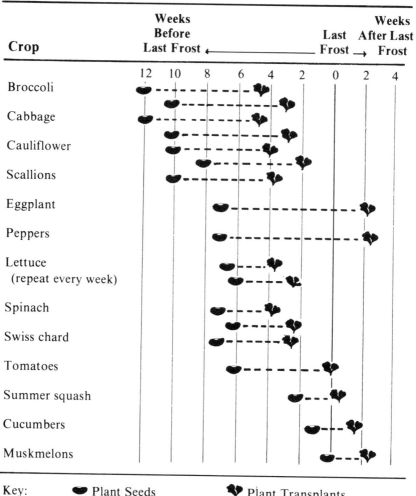

Crop	Weeks Before Last Frost ←	Last Frost →	Weeks After Last Frost

Broccoli

Cabbage

Cauliflower

Scallions

Eggplant

Peppers

Lettuce
(repeat every week)

Spinach

Swiss chard

Tomatoes

Summer squash

Cucumbers

Muskmelons

Key: 🫘 Plant Seeds   🌱 Plant Transplants
             --- Indoor Growing Time
Each numbered block stands for 2 weeks

FALL PLANTING SCHEDULE FOR LAST CROPS

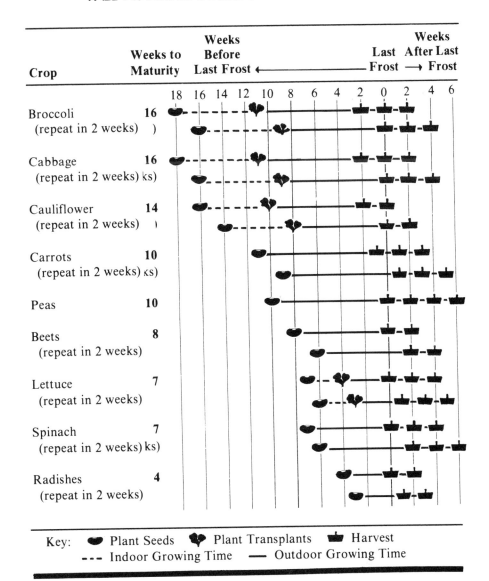

Crop	Weeks to Maturity	Weeks Before Last Frost ←	————	Last Frost →	Weeks After Last Frost

Broccoli — 16
(repeat in 2 weeks))

Cabbage — 16
(repeat in 2 weeks) ks)

Cauliflower — 14
(repeat in 2 weeks))

Carrots — 10
(repeat in 2 weeks) ks)

Peas — 10

Beets — 8
(repeat in 2 weeks)

Lettuce — 7
(repeat in 2 weeks)

Spinach — 7
(repeat in 2 weeks) ks)

Radishes — 4
(repeat in 2 weeks)

Key: ● Plant Seeds ♥ Plant Transplants ⛴ Harvest
--- Indoor Growing Time — Outdoor Growing Time

OUTDOOR PLANTING SCHEDULE
FOR A CONTINUOUS CROP

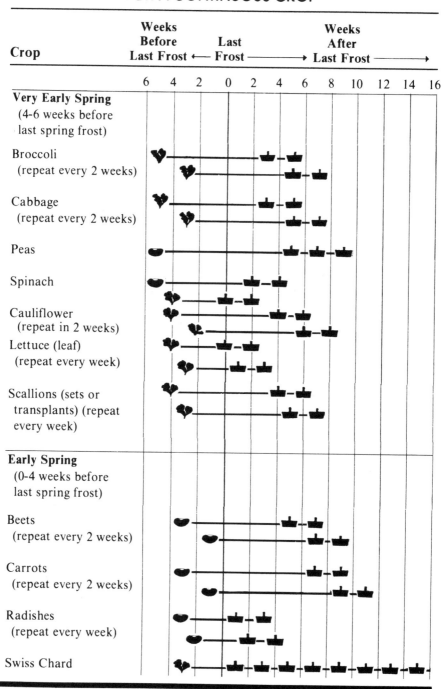

Crop	Weeks Before Last Frost ←	Last Frost →	Weeks After Last Frost →

Very Early Spring
(4-6 weeks before
last spring frost)

Broccoli
(repeat every 2 weeks)

Cabbage
(repeat every 2 weeks)

Peas

Spinach

Cauliflower
(repeat in 2 weeks)

Lettuce (leaf)
(repeat every week)

Scallions (sets or
transplants) (repeat
every week)

Early Spring
(0-4 weeks before
last spring frost)

Beets
(repeat every 2 weeks)

Carrots
(repeat every 2 weeks)

Radishes
(repeat every week)

Swiss Chard

OUTDOOR PLANTING SCHEDULE
FOR A CONTINUOUS CROP

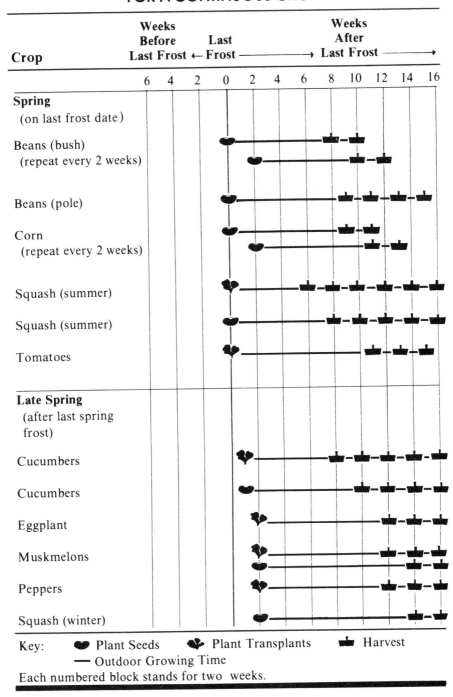

Crop	Weeks Before Last Frost		Last Frost →		Weeks After Last Frost →							
	6	4	2	0	2	4	6	8	10	12	14	16

Spring
(on last frost date)

Beans (bush)
(repeat every 2 weeks)

Beans (pole)

Corn
(repeat every 2 weeks)

Squash (summer)

Squash (summer)

Tomatoes

Late Spring
(after last spring frost)

Cucumbers

Cucumbers

Eggplant

Muskmelons

Peppers

Squash (winter)

Key: 🫘 Plant Seeds   🌱 Plant Transplants   ⛵ Harvest
— Outdoor Growing Time
Each numbered block stands for two weeks.

Spacing Plan

The next step is to start thinking about a spacing plan. Since you'll be planting more than one square foot of each crop at a time, think in terms of the total number of plants to one, two, three, or four linear feet of bed. You'll find the arithmetic is extremely easy. For example, if you're putting in extra-large plants at a spacing of one per square foot, you'll be putting in four plants for every linear foot of your bed.

The next size would be plants which are spaced four per square foot, or sixteen per linear foot of bed. The medium-sized plants require a spacing of nine per square foot, for a total of thirty-six per linear foot of bed. The small plants such as radishes and carrots fit sixteen per square foot or a total of sixty-four plants per linear foot of bed. After a while these numbers will become second nature to you and you won't have to figure them out on paper or even stop to think about them. And if you take the trouble to lay out your beds on graph paper, allowing one square per square foot, you'll find it very easy to count and measure.

Weather Protection

Next, consider your ability to provide frost protection. If you're starting during the cool season, decide how much that's going to play in your decision to gamble and start early or play it safe. You may not be home enough to put on the covers, or you may be unwilling to put in that much time and effort.

If you're starting your garden during the hot season, you must decide how much weather protection you're going to provide, such as shade film, wind screens, and heavy rain protection. A lot depends upon your area of the country and the typical weather you can expect during each season. Make your plan to fit your particular weather conditions. For example, some areas of the country receive drying winds all summer long. Other areas lack in sunshine and the air is still but very humid. If your area is windy, you should provide some sort of wind screen and some ground cover or mulching system to hold the moisture. But if it's cloudy and humid, you should make sure there's nothing to hold in the dampness or block out any drying sunlight, which will cause rotting and mildew.

It's easy to add a clear plastic cover when a wire framework is in place. Plastic will protect against those early spring frosts.

Don't schedule the entire year all at once. You'll find that your crops will grow more quickly or slowly than you anticipated, your weather will be different from last year, and you might spend a lot of time and work on a chart that could be obsolete in a couple of months. Start with the first few months. Get your crops started, the quick crops replanted, and the summer crops planted and into their first harvest. Later, you can compare your projected charts with your actual harvest records to see how close your estimates were. Make note of the discrepancies. This will help you with next year's crop schedules.

Vacation Time

One last consideration in planting is your vacation. How long do you plan to be away, and what happens to your harvest and planting schedule then? Also, do you want to make a break in your deliveries, or do you want to train someone to take over for you? Maybe you're having so much fun that you want to stay home this year. At the same time, you might want to check on your buyer's vacation. It's possible he may close for a week or two in the summer. Even if he's open year-round, you should find out when he expects to go on vacation. Review everything with his replacement so you can avoid problems while he's away.

What You'll Buy

Your last task is to estimate the quantities of seed or transplants you'll need for the season. Do you plan to purchase transplants from a local nursery? Do you want the nursery to order any special varieties for you?

Unless you're planning an extremely large garden, it won't pay you to buy the jumbo packets of seeds the first year. If you buy too many at once, you may wind up with enough to last for several years. You may also want to change varieties after the first year, or the seed companies may come out with a variety more suited to your needs, and you'll want to try those seeds instead of the ones you saved.

If you do have seeds left over—and they test for viability—there's no reason why you shouldn't use them. Test them as explained here. If the germination rate has dropped to 50 percent, you have to double the number of seeds that you plant. Often the older seeds take longer to sprout, so you have to give them a little extra time. But since square foot gardening uses a controlled method of planting very few seeds, you should have no problem.

Finally, on the choice of seeds, use only the best varieties, and seeds you're sure are viable. Don't economize foolishly where your business is concerned.

A final suggestion: show your neatly finished charts to someone else—your spouse, a neighbor, or a gardening friend. You might even take them to your buyer. The purpose of this is to see if they can be understood, and to generate suggestions. Quite often we get so close to something that we're working on that we forget some of the obvious things.

HOW TO TEST FOR GERMINATION

Here's an easy and quick method to test whether those seeds you saved should be planted in this year's garden.

Dampen a paper towel. Fold it once and place exactly ten seeds on it. Fold it again and wrap it in a dampened folded face towel. Place the towel in a saucer or plate. Mark it with the variety of seeds, and the date. Keep it in a warm place, such as near the hot water tank.

Keep moist but remember that seeds need both moisture and air to prevent rotting, so don't keep sopping wet.

Open every few days to inspect. Most seeds will sprout within seven to ten days.

Count the number of seeds that sprouted, and multiply that number by ten. That's the percentage of germination. A germination rate of 40 to 50 percent is poor, but still usable. Germination rates of 60 to 70 percent are good, while 80 and above are excellent.

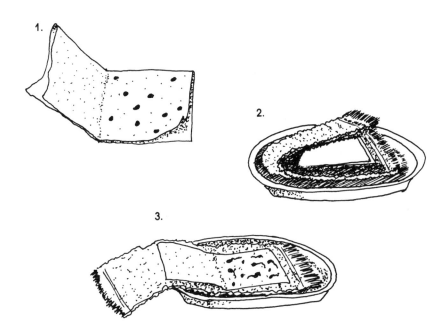

1.

2.

3.

Drawing Charts

Draw your charts on 8½ x 11 paper so you can make Xerox copies for later use. Make them neat, and write dark enough so they'll reproduce well.

The charts in this chapter tell you when to start everything according to your frost dates. The charts and information in the next chapter will help you to lay out how much garden space is needed for your desired harvest.

By combining the information in both chapters, you'll have a plan laid out that tells you:

> 1. When to plant
>   a. Seeds indoors
>   b. Seeds outdoors
>   c. Transplants outdoors
>
> 2. How much to plant
>
> 3. How often to replant
>
> 4. How much garden space is needed.

STARTING TIMES

Your Last Frost Date

Crop	Weeks Before Last Frost to Start Seeds Indoors	Date to Start Seeds Indoors	Date to Start Seeds Outdoors	Date to Put Trans- plants Out
Continuous Harvest				
Cucumbers				
Eggplants				
Peppers				
Squash				
Swiss chard				
Tomatoes				
Limited Harvest				
Pole beans				
Bush beans				
Peas				
Single Harvest *Seeded Indoors*				
Broccoli				
Cabbage				
Cauliflower				
Lettuce				
Spinach				
Single Harvest *Seeded Outdoors*				
Beets				
Radishes				
Turnips				
Scallions				

Chapter 13
Start Planting

Planting consists of three steps:

1. Starting seeds indoors, transplanting seedlings into individual containers, then growing the transplants.

2. Planting these transplants in the garden when it's warm enough.

3. Planting seeds directly into the garden.

Of course, you could skip step 1 and buy your transplants at a local nursery. More than likely, you'll want to start your own for your cash garden. You'll save money, and get a better choice of varieties.

The reason many crops are started as transplants is to save time. As soon as the weather is warm enough, gardeners want to get off to a fast start by putting in plants rather than seeds. But some crops don't transplant well, or they have seeds that sprout so quickly that there's no advantage to growing transplants.

Before it's time to start the seeds, set up a schedule. How detailed it should be will depend on you. You can keep elaborate charts, or you can scrawl notations on the back of an envelope. You should figure out (and the accompanying charts should help you) when to start your seeds, indoors or out, how many to start at a time, and how often to start a new batch for succession crops.

List all the crops you plan to grow. For those that have a continuous harvest (tomatoes, peppers, cucumbers), decide how many plants you'll need. Get your last spring frost date from chapter twelve, enter it on your schedule, and figure out when you should start the seeds.

For those crops grown for a limited harvest over a few weeks (beans, peas), decide how many plants you'll need and how often you'll have to replant.

For those crops that are grown for a single harvest (lettuce, carrots, radishes), decide how many plants you'll need weekly for your restaurant. Using the typical square foot spacing, fill in the number of square feet you need of each crop. Find the number of weeks to harvest and multiply that number by the weekly crop space requirement. For example, if you want fifty to sixty radishes a week, you'll have to plant four square feet weekly (4 X 16 = 64). Since radishes mature in four weeks, you'll need four weeks of space or four different crops going at once. That means you'll need 4 (weeks) X 4 (square feet) = 16 square feet of garden space just for radishes.

In cooler weather, everything grows more slowly, so you might add a fifth week of planting, thus boosting your space requirement for radishes to twenty square feet.

Use the same method to work out the space requirements for a crop that needs transplants on a weekly schedule, such as lettuce, but also determine how many seeds to start each week. Figure on about thirty seeds to get twenty seedlings, and transplant those twenty to get sixteen good transplants. These numbers are just calculated guesses based on experience, age of seeds, and success with growing transplants. Some seeds have a much lower percentage of germination, so you will have to plant more to get the required number of seedlings. You'll learn as you work with them.

Now you know how much garden space you need to harvest the crops you need, how many seeds to start indoors and outdoors, and when you should start them. After you do this once or twice, you'll see it's very easy. If you're not good at math or don't like charts or lists, don't worry. Many people do all this on the back of an envelope. (Well, maybe two envelopes.)

Starting Seeds Indoors

Make sure you have the right conditions and equipment for starting seeds indoors.

You should have a sunny area, preferably a greenhouse or a place with light coming from above. Many people believe that a window with a southern exposure is ideal. They end up with a lot of leggy plants leaning toward that window.

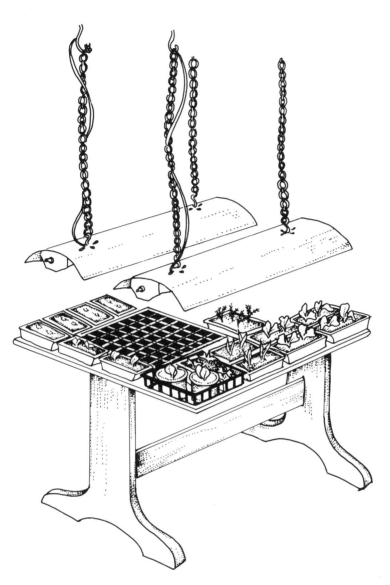

For stocky, healthy transplants, it's hard to beat this lighting system.

If you don't have a greenhouse or overhead sunlight, you can grow your transplants indoors under lights. The seeds can be germinated in darkness, but must be moved into full light the minute they sprout. You can construct a fairly simple setup with fluorescent lights. It must be adjustable so the lights can be brought down very close to the plants, then kept several inches above their tops as they grow.

Temperature

You need a controlled temperature of about 70° F., twenty-four hours a day, for germination. That temperature is too warm for the plants or seedlings, and causes them to grow too quickly and become leggy. Ideally, you'll start your seeds at 70°, then move the tiny plants under the fluorescent lights where temperatures of 50° at night and 60° in the daytime can be maintained.

The procedure for cash gardening is the same as was described in chapter three, except that for a cash garden, you'll be starting far more seeds.

Planting Outdoors

For those seeds that you're going to plant outdoors, it's just a matter of deciding when it's safe to plant them. The charts in chapter twelve will give you a general idea, and your observation of the weather will help you to make up your mind.

It's worthwhile in early spring to help the soil warm up by covering the beds with clear plastic. Then you can plant your seeds and cover the bed with one of the wire and plastic bed covers. You'll want to be careful to vent these devices so the heat doesn't build up and cook the young plants.

These precautions are just for the early crops. Later plantings will need a different kind of protection, from drying out or being washed out by heavy rains. Covers help for both of these.

Replanting

Once you start harvesting, you'll have empty squares. When should you replant them? Immediately upon harvest. As an example, you are harvesting bibb lettuce and every week four square feet are available for replanting. Since rotating your crops makes sense, you'd probably put in a root crop next, something that requires different nutrients.

Let's say you need thirty carrots a week—two square feet of them. The lettuce gives up four square feet every week, you'll have carrots in two square feet—and two more feet of space. You could assign that space to another fast-growing crop such as radishes, but don't worry too much about small spaces, since it will all balance out with another crop in a few weeks.

Some people have suggested the use of a personal computer to figure out how to best utilize space. If you have one (I don't yet), and you're into that sort of thing, go ahead. But for you who don't, don't be scared off. There is no need for rigid rules, and succession crops don't have to be planted near each other.

One last word about planting charts. You don't have to project the exact number of plants that you should plant and harvest, if you follow the marketing advice in chapter four. If you convince your buyer to take whatever you have because you're going to give him only your best, you don't have to bring him an exact amount every week. If you're a little short of one item, you might have extra of another. This allows you to make the maximum profit from every square foot and to have little, if any, waste.

Transplanting

The last step in preparing your garden is moving your transplants out. Check the frost charts to make sure it is safe. Consult your garden charts to see where to plant each variety. Have all your equipment ready. Have a bucket of warm water, a cup, a trowel, any spacing device you have constructed, a kneeling pad, sunshades to put over the plants, and any pest controls.

Chicken wire cages are useful against rabbits; for protection against birds and other pests, cover your wooden frames with bird netting or screening.

This chicken-wire cage will protect your crops from rabbits and birds.

(One of the easiest ways to grow organically is to provide a fine-mesh screened cover so insects can't get into the crop to lay their eggs.)

The best day for transplanting is the day before you can be around your garden all day. The second day is critical for transplants, and you should keep an eye on them.

Since you'll be using protective cages for your transplants, the time of day when you put them out isn't as critical as it is in conventional gardening. However, the best time of day is in mid-afternoon, when the sun is losing its intensity. Mid-morning is not as good, because the plant is subject to strong sunlight and heat for the rest of the day. Early evening is not bad, but you are subjecting the plant to cooler temperatures very soon after transplanting.

Don't plant in strong sunlight, or if you have to, shade the area with your body as you plant. Give the plants a drink of water as soon as you put them in the ground. And put up sunshades, and wind protection if needed, as soon as you've completed your planting.

Protection during the next week is critical. Your sunshades should stay up for one to three days, depending on the weather and time of year.

And you should look over your young transplants daily. In a square foot garden, that's easy. You're usually out there every day, and it doesn't take long to check over a small garden.

Early spring lettuce is protected by this wire cage.

Chapter 14
Growing

$\boxed{\$}$ Given the ideal soil (which you should now have), sufficient moisture (which you can easily provide), and protection from pests (which you can also provide), the only other thing your crops need to perform to their maximum is good weather. For that you must say a few prayers, knock on wood every morning, or use your own secret formula to get Mother Nature to cooperate. Ultimately, I think you'll find her to be an independent soul who's not easily influenced. Let's concentrate instead on what you can do for your garden, and leave her to her own devices.

Watering

In your cash garden, keep your plants growing as fast as possible. Don't let them go through dry spells or get to the point of wilting. This will subject them to water stress, which not only affects their rate of growth, but in most cases alters their taste. It produces bitter lettuce, coarse radishes, tough carrots, and tasteless tomatoes and corn. Water stress occurs when the plant can't take up enough moisture from the roots to the leaves. This can happen on a very hot day when the sun is drying the moisture out of the leaves faster than the roots can replenish it. It can also occur even when the sun isn't out, if you are having a dry spell with little moisture in the soil.

To avoid water stress, set up a regular watering schedule. I recommend dipping sun-warmed water by hand from a bucket. Since your garden will be much larger than a typical square foot garden, you'll need a couple of buckets. One trick to having enough

These are the tools for watering. A pail and a cup are fine for individual plants such as lettuce and cabbages. For more extensive watering, use a hose with a spray nozzle and a shut-off valve near the nozzle.

warm water is to leave a hose coiled up in the sun, have it dripping into one bucket while you're using another, and have a third in reserve. With three buckets you should have no trouble keeping ahead of the game and having a full bucket ready at all times.

If you live in a very hot climate, have sandy soil, or have a very large garden, you might want to form your soil into the hill-and-furrow shape described earlier. This can be done with or without the paper mulch described. Now it's very easy to water using a hose extender, shut-off valve, and spray nozzle. Just move the nozzle up and down each furrow. Your shut-off valve can be adjusted so the water pressure won't wash the soil or young plants away. By coiling an extra length of hose in the sun, you'll get warmer water so the plants aren't put into shock.

Watch Your Plants

Take advantage of the time you spend watering to get close to your plants. Be observant. Look for any pest damage; determine if the plant is ready for harvest; notice growth, soil conditions, and anything else that may affect your garden. One advantage a square foot garden has over a single row garden is that it is so small that you have time to look at each individual plant as you water it by hand.

Too much moisture can also damage your crops. While it's unlikely that you'll actually overwater them, it is possible to have too much rain. Then it's time to throw on those wire cages and cover them with clear plastic. This keeps out all the moisture but lets in the air and light. (Don't cover the sides, just the top.) This technique will help your soil drain. Since you provided that perfect soil, it should drain quickly. Your plants will not become waterlogged and they'll continue to grow in the light that's available.

If too much rain is a problem, protect your plants with a sheet of plastic.

Fertilizing

This is not to be confused with the fertilizing you did as part of your initial soil preparation. Every crop is slightly different and requires extra fertilizer, depending on the length of time it spends in the ground before harvest. Vegetables that are ready for harvest within six weeks really don't need anything beyond initial soil preparation. Beyond that, it usually pays to apply fertilizer about the sixth week.

Be sure to pick a strength and formula that are suitable to your crop. For example, on the NPK ratio (nitrogen-phosphorus-potassium) pick something that is high in N for lettuce, high in P for fruit crops, and high in K for root crops.

The crops that stay in the ground more than six weeks should be fertilized at least once a month after your initial soil preparation. An even better method would be to apply a half-strength solution of fertilizer every other week. This doles out the food in a strength that's a little easier for the plants to take up. Any vegetable that has a blossom should get an extra application of high P fertilizer at the blossoming time. If you're using a granular fertilizer, many books will tell you to scratch it into the surface. However, this can sometimes disturb the roots of the plants. The method I like to use is to mix the granular fertilizer with an equal amount of compost, which helps to spread it out. Then just sprinkle the mixture around the base of the plants. The compost also acts as a buffering agent, storing up the nutrients and releasing them a little more slowly.

Weeding

This is a very short subject in a square foot gardening book, because a square foot garden has very short weeds. If you weed while you water (at least once a week), you'll never have any weeds in your garden that are more than one week old...mere babes in arms. Just think, no weeds to compete with your plants for sun, moisture, nutrients, and space. This is probably one of the most appreciated features of a square foot garden. At first people are skeptical. They can't imagine it. But then I get so many letters saying how easy it is to keep the garden perfectly weeded that I know the readers have been convinced.

Don't let the weeds grow in your walking aisles. Lay down boards or use an action hoe weekly, grow grass and mow weekly, or cover the surface with a protective mulch.

Pests

Since your crops are practically cash in the bank, you don't want to lose any of them to pests. Be on the watch for slugs, cutworms, rabbits, or anything that could get to your crops before you do. Put up those protective cages ahead of time. Even more important, check your garden daily. Learn to look for unusual situations.

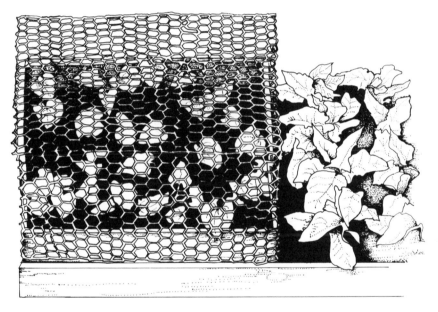

A wooden frame covered with chicken wire offers the most positive protection from hungry rabbits.

Develop the ability to spot trouble before it happens. For example, a blank spot in the garden; leaves that are droopy, half-eaten, or have holes or ragged edges; silver trails from slugs and snails who visited the night before—all are warning signals that can be detected by an observant gardener. A square foot gardener, that is. A conventional, single row garden can't be observed this closely because it's just too big.

Peppers grow up through the wire frame for support. Add the wire when plants are half-grown, bending it to the shape and height desired. The wire can be the same size that you used for growing tomatoes vertically.

Supports

Another way to keep your work load down and your production up is to provide supports for your plants. Oh, I don't mean stakes and ties and all that stuff. Just stretch some large-opening wire mesh over each bed when the plants are still small and staple it to the wooden frames; they'll grow right through it and support themselves. Then let *them* do the work .... you just take it easy.

Think ahead; try to picture the plants that usually fall over when they're full grown and heavy with harvest (peppers and eggplants, to name two). These are the crops that will need a helping hand. Of course all your vertical crops are being supported by the same wire, except they're growing straight up on their vertical frames.

Mulching

If you could assure your soil of constant moisture and adequate nutrients, if you could keep it weed-free and protected from pounding rains or the baking sun, if you could maintain a more even temperature throughout each day, your plants would produce much better. How to accomplish all that? Put a mulch down. Mulch is defined as any material that comes between your soil and the weather. Once your plants are established, a layer of almost any kind of material will provide a buffer to break up the force of the rain; it will also protect the soil from the drying effects of the sun and act as insulation to keep the soil's temperature more uniform. Many organic materials, such as hay, chopped leaves, or dried grass clippings, are free or inexpensive to buy. Many man-made materials, such as black plastic and outdoor carpeting, do just as good a job and look even neater. The organic materials have the added advantage of gradually decomposing and adding even more nutrients and humus to the soil. They should be applied as soon as the soil warms up and your plants are in the ground.

Mulch between your beds will prevent weeds from growing there.

Maintains Even Moisture

Another big advantage of mulching is that it maintains an even moisture level in the soil. When the weather is hot, the ground moisture doesn't evaporate as quickly; when it rains, the water doesn't flood the soil, but filters through the mulch at a slower rate.

Many people believe that mulch, which creates cool, moist conditions, will attract slugs, crickets, and other bugs. This question has caused controversy among the experts. In my garden, I have never experienced an increase in any of the "bad" bugs due to the use of mulch. In fact, I've experimented side-by-side with and without mulch and could really see no difference as far as pest damage was concerned.

One good thing the mulch *will* attract is earthworms. They love the cool, moist conditions and will spend more time tunneling through your soil digesting all that compost and turning it into even richer material.

Growing Lettuce

What if your plants get too much sun, or it's too hot for them to grow, as with lettuce, which quickly bolts to seed in the summer? Well, with just a little common sense and ingenuity, you can grow lettuce in just about any part of the country, even in the summer. That is hard to believe at first, but it's very easy to do. Let's imagine that it's you and not the lettuce who's sitting in the garden all day under the hot summer sun. What could I get for you? Some shade, and a drink, and some cool soil to dig your feet into. So all you have to do is grow your lettuce under a shade film supported by one of those wire cages. Make sure you plant in a saucer-shaped depression, provide perfect soil which drains well and is filled with moisture-holding humus, cover that soil with a thick mulch to keep out the hot sun, and water about twice as often as usual. You'll see that it can be done.

While I was in Florida giving a lecture, a lady came up to me and said she followed all the advice in my first book and was now able to grow lettuce in Florida in the middle of the summer. Everyone listened, not unappreciatively, but I think they were shaking their heads. But she knows that it can be done, and you will too. What's more, just think how it will improve your profits.

FLORIDA LETTUCE

I asked a good friend in Orlando, Florida, to try the cash garden idea so that we would know if it would work in yet another part of the country.

He planted just lettuce, since he is a manager of a large nursery and has very few hours to spare at home.

By having a weekly supply of seedlings and transplants coming along, he was able to grow lettuce that could be harvested after just four weeks in the garden.

And it looked so good that his buyer paid him $1 a head.

At four heads per square foot, that's $4 per square foot per month. Each four-foot by four-foot area in the garden was producing $64 a month. Ten areas, or two beds 4 x 20 feet each, isn't a very large area, but it would produce $640 a month. Not bad for just a few hours of work a week.

Cultivating

My last piece of advice concerns something everyone used to have to do in the old-fashioned, single row garden—get out and hoe and cultivate, chop down those weeds, loosen up that soil, and hill up those plants, all in a three-foot-wide aisle. It was a terribly hot, dusty, dirty job.

But in a square foot garden, you *never* have to cultivate. Why? Because you've never walked on your growing soil to pack it down. Therefore, it never needs loosening up. You pull the weeds by hand when they are only an inch or so high, so you don't need a big, heavy hoe. And you have perfect growing soil that is already friable, loose, and filled with humus, so there is no need to cultivate to let the air in. Since you have so much humus, it will attract a lot of earthworms which will loosen it and aerate it even further. And if you mulch, it won't get baked hard and crusty in the sun like an overdone pie.

If it all sounds too easy to be true, try it and see. The square foot system will take you through your growing season with a minimum of effort, leaving you with lots of time for harvesting and delivering your produce, and going to the bank with your profits.

Chapter 15
Harvesting

$\boxed{\$}$ This step in the process of running your business can be very time-consuming if you don't work efficiently. It can also be disastrous if done incorrectly. Yet it is one of the most rewarding steps. All your hard work and planning have finally culminated in the harvest.

Everyone loves to pick vegetables, and when they're all washed and arranged, they make a memorable picture. To make sure it's really memorable, take some pictures during harvesting and delivery. Some should be action photos of yourself at work in your garden or loading the harvest into your vehicle. They're nice to have when you're lining up prospective customers. You can show your pictures at any time; no need to wait for the harvest season to pick a basket. In fact, a picture of the garden might even be better because it will show the volume you are able to produce. A restaurant owner will then understand how you can produce so much week after week.

When

I recommend harvesting in the morning before the sun gets to the plants. You might have read books that advise you to harvest after the sun dries out the morning dew, or in the late afternoon when the heat of the day is over. Sometimes it depends on the particular vegetable, but quite often it depends on the gardener's preference. When it comes to practicality, it usually depends on your schedule.

And don't forget the restaurant. It may have hours when it likes delivery.

If you remember the agreement you drew up with your customer (chapter four), you'll recall that you promised delivery within two hours of picking. That eliminates an evening session in the garden. Next, I think you should consider your temperament. If you don't like to get up early, you're going to be unhappy having to get up at 6 twice a week to deliver to the restaurant at 10:30. It would be better to rig up some protection from the noonday sun and promise delivery at 1 so you can snooze until 9 and enjoy your harvesting. Ideally, of course, most people like to get up at 6, be outdoors working by 7, enjoy the cool, clear air, and be all finished by late morning. If you work, and cash gardening is a part-time supplement to your income, then of course your regular working hours will determine when you can harvest and deliver.

Fresher in Morning

So much for *your* preferences. But what about those of your vegetables? For most, morning is the best time to harvest, if for no other reason than that they're more moisture-laden, weigh more, and are crisper and fresher. After a hot day, most leafy vegetables have lost a lot of moisture to the atmosphere and may even be a little wilted. There are very few that build up sugars (hence sweetness) in the daytime. Corn is one of them; tomatoes another. Of course corn should be picked as close to mealtime as possible, while tomatoes can hold over for many hours, if not days, without deteriorating. Aside from these two exceptions, the general rule of thumb is to harvest in the morning.

What

The next question is, "What to harvest?" If you did a good job of selling your services and negotiating an agreement; you can now pick whatever's ready and sell it all. It's wise to keep an eye ahead to the next harvest or two as well. For example, let's say that all of your ruby lettuce has not quite matured, but the weather is getting very hot and you see a few of the early plants starting to elongate. This means that they're all going to bolt to seed before reaching maturity. So you should keep them well-watered and shaded, and harvest as much as you can for your next delivery without overloading it.

Keep an eye on the weather as well. The maturity of plants depends heavily on the weather, especially on sunlight and heat. You could keep a close watch on the five-day weather forecast, but frankly I've found it changes so much every few days that it's not worth worrying about. I'd rather rely on a little common sense than the long-range forecast. It's better to pick most things a little early and small than it is to let them get bigger and risk their becoming tough or bitter. You can't afford to deliver tough or bitter produce. Get in the habit of tasting your vegetables frequently while you pick them. Look for toughness, bitterness, pithiness, dryness, and all the things we don't want associated with cash gardening. (Hint: oversized vegetables usually taste inferior, so don't include these in your harvest. Consider them "seconds.")

If you are going to have an abundance of any item, be sure to mention it in advance to the owner or head chef. That way he can plan his menu around it, and you can still sell it.

Picking Order

Does it matter in what order you pick your vegetables? You'd better believe it! Consider how long each one takes to harvest, wash, and clean, and how fragile it is. You certainly don't want to pick your delicate lettuce first (even if it takes the longest) and let it sit around for two hours while you harvest everything else. Some small things, such as parsley or beans, can be harvested first and put in the refrigerator or cooler. String beans take a long time to harvest but take up little room. You might also have a small amount of spinach—enough to fill up a shopping bag or two—so that could fit in the cooler as well.

Root vegetables take a little time and have to be cleaned, but they don't take up much room and can be left *in water.* Have an extra pail or two, or an old ice chest. Styrofoam picnic chests can be purchased very cheaply, or you can make your own by gluing a few sheets of styrofoam together and putting them in a heavy plastic bag. Fill with water, drop in a chunk of ice, and you're set with storage for root crops for hours.

Lettuce will be the bulkiest of your crops. You'll probably have case after case of several varieties. If you have a real problem keeping things cool while you harvest, try digging a ground pit big enough to store several crates. The ground is very cool if you go down four to five feet. The ideal one would have a side entrance and an earth cover. You'll find it also serves a special purpose in the fall and winter for storing root crops with protection from freezing. If it's close to your garden area, it will be just as handy in summer as in winter.

Tools

To harvest quickly and efficiently, make sure you have the proper picking tools, boxes, pails, and flats. Part of picking quickly and efficiently depends on your equipment. Don't try to get by with just the knife or pocket clipper you'd use in your square foot garden. Cash gardening is a whole different business. Just as you needed proper equipment for seed sprouting and planting, when operating on a large scale you must have efficient harvesting equipment. Since you'll be handling a large volume, think of things that will simplify, consolidate, and eliminate movement. Keep everything handy and close by so you won't have to walk twenty feet to empty a small basket into a large one.

The first handy harvest aid I recommend is a cart or wheelbarrow that will fit in your walking paths. If you have an old-fashioned wheelbarrow with a flat bed you can use it in the paths without too much trouble.

You need several strong pails. Stay away from the $1.49 variety and invest in at least two heavy-duty plastic pails. They'll last a long time and won't crack or break at a critical moment.

Your hose system should extend to all parts of the garden and have shut-off valves at several strategic locations so you don't have to walk back and forth a lot just to fill a pail.

Packing Boxes for Free

Boxes and flats are free for the asking at any grocery store. Wood flats, crates, and even good bushel baskets are thrown out every day. Ask the produce department manager if you can pick up a few each week, and you'll have a good collection in no time. Since they break and wear out, get extras.

You might also consider shallow cardboard boxes, the kind used in beverage stores for soda and beer. These are ideal because you can't pack too much in them and risk crushing your fruit, yet you can dispose of them at the restaurant if you don't want to bring them home.

It's often possible to get boxes and crates free from a grocery store.

Of course, cardboard doesn't have the professional "farm-grown" look of wood flats, so you may want to stick with the latter until you've made your first impression. The other problem with cardboard is its unsuitability during wet weather, and that's the same problem you'll have with paper bags. The nice thing about wood boxes is that you can use them in any weather; in fact, you can hose down your produce right in the boxes.

Picking aids are the next major category to consider. You *must* have several good clippers that are easy to open and close. Why several? Well, if you're like me, you're always misplacing tools. Although I make New Year's resolutions all the time about being better organized, I've found the easiest solution is to buy three of any hand tool once I find one I like. A good strong pocket knife is also very useful every day. For cutting things such as lettuce and Swiss chard, an old, inexpensive, steak knife with a serrated blade is the handiest tool.

Those are the basics. Other specialized items you could investigate and buy are picking bags, pails, and other harvesting devices. Any commercial orchard catalog will feature them.

Harvesting Techniques

Let's start with the *root crops*. Have two pails close at hand, filled with clean water. Make sure your hose is turned on and you have a shut-off at the hose end where you're working. Get down on your knees and start down the path. Using two hands, pull whatever is ready till you have five in each hand. Combine them, then dunk and wash them in one bucket until they're fairly clean. Pick off all dead or yellow leaves and cull out any undersized vegetables. Rinse them in the second bucket. Count and place them in the flat next to you. Repeat, but keep the count and add to it only after you wash and rinse. We've tried counting ten and placing one in a box to represent those ten, or counting by ones as each ten are picked or washed, but in the long run it's much less confusing to simply say what you have as you place it in the flat: "10-20-30." By combining both bunches of five in one hand, you can rub, scrub with a brush, and pick off dead leaves with the other.

As soon as your rinse water gets dirty, change your buckets. How can you do that and cut your bucket-filling in half? By using the rinse water bucket as the next wash water bucket. Empty the original wash water bucket and fill it with clean water. It becomes the new rinse bucket. Don't spill the wash water into the paths (your knees will get soaked) or the beds you're still working in. Water the tomatoes and cucumbers where you have dug deep watering troughs. Then you won't wash away any tender plants and you won't waste time slowly emptying the bucket.

Pull Everything in Sight

With some vegetables you may find it easier to harvest everything and throw away those that are too small rather than taking the time to pull the foliage aside, inspect the root crown, and decide whether to pull or spare the plant. Radishes are a good example. Since they only take three to four weeks, they all mature fairly close together. If the restaurant doesn't mind, give them small, medium, and large— unsorted, if possible. Tell them you'll throw in the smallest ones at no cost so they don't think they're being cheated. Or pick them all and sort them into small, medium, and large for delivery. This will take more time, but they'll look much better that way.

Don't let the tops of root vegetables get tangled so you have to pull and separate each one. Like combing long hair after it's been washed and is all knotted together, this is very time-consuming.

Another thing to consider is how many undersized plants you must leave in the ground to justify the use of that land for another week. If you have another crop to put in, it might pay to pull everything, sort it, and sell the small plants for half price (or use them at your table) and go on to the next crop.

Cut the Tops?

Before delivering, should you break the tops off? The advantages of removing them are that you can use the tops for mulch and much-needed organic matter in your compost pile, and that the harvest now takes up half the room it did before, which facilitates delivery and storage.

The disadvantage is that you've lost that home-grown look. Your beets, stripped of their colorful tops, look naked and forlorn, and your delivery now looks just like any other tub of beets: no class, no color, no pizzazz. So leave the tops on. In fact, do everything you can to make that harvest look as if it belongs at the county fair with a blue ribbon on it. That's salesmanship. That's one of the things you need to learn to insure a successful business.

It would also take more of your time to trim the tops off, and the restaurant may want to use those tops. Beet tops, at least, are edible, and the smaller leaves are delicious either raw in salads, cooked as greens, or in soups or stews for flavor and color.

Compost Pile Matter

What's more, those tops are not necessarily lost to you even if they're delivered to the restaurant. Usually a restaurant prepares its vegetables in a separate room, or at least in a separate sink. Why not ask the chef if you can remove all his vegetable leavings each time you deliver? He might even offer to pay you to take them away. But if you volunteer to do it free of charge, how can he turn you down? It's hard to find such high-quality organic matter, so look at those peelings and tops as gold to be added to your soil.

The only drawback is the polluting matter, which the workers may throw in, such as cigarette butts, styrofoam cups, and plastic wrappers. If you do arrange to haul this material away, tell the help how important it is to keep the trimmings clean. Ask them to throw all trimmings in a separate box or can, which you can provide. Label it with a sign: **VEGETABLE MATTER ONLY**

You might also provide a sign that says: **MAN-MADE TRASH**

for the regular can to avoid confusion.

Leaf Crops

Our next category is *leaf crops*—including lettuce, spinach, and Swiss chard. Since you can offer varieties that farmers and suppliers can't, you should grow a lot of greens, especially the leaf and fancy types of lettuce. Most restaurants like a wide variety for a mixed green salad. Your growing plan should take this into account so you have a good variety to harvest each week.

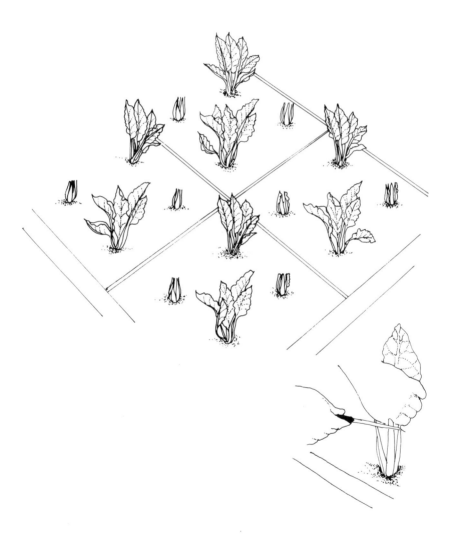

A very efficient way to harvest leaf crops is to cut the entire head. Some plants, like Swiss chard and parsley, will start growing again. To get maximum use of your garden space, cut every other head.

Another advantage is that you can plant fairly close together because you can harvest every other plant in a checkerboard pattern. This leaves room for the remaining plants to mature. By the time this happens, your first set of plants has grown back halfway. Now, when you harvest the second set, the first set has room to finish growing without crowding. This method works so well on Swiss chard and parsley that you'll never have to replant all year. Your bed will just keep producing crop after crop, sometimes up to four or six cuttings a season.

Use a serrated knife when harvesting lettuce. Cut it as close to the ground as possible. Leave the stump and root, and avoid getting dirt on the lettuce. Remove the roots later when preparing the bed for a new crop.

Steak Knife Handy

An inexpensive serrated steak knife is the handiest tool for cutting the heads. Some like to use strong grass shears or a pair of clippers that opens wide. As with your root crops, keep two buckets close by for washing and rinsing, and keep all tools and equipment beside or behind you in the path. Pick off any yellow or dead leaves and drop them into a bucket or box to be thrown on the mulch pile, or leave them in the bed to be turned under. (Leaving them in the path to decompose gives the garden a messy appearance.) Since they might contain slugs, sowbugs, or other pests, I like to remove them to the mulch pile. It's a little more work, but it's worthwhile and it keeps the garden looking neat.

Have your washing and rinsing buckets handy when you harvest root
and salad crops.

Keep count as you rinse and pack the heads in the flat. Some ask
whether a crate can be used (the kind with thin wood joined by
wire). You certainly can pack more into a crate, but it doesn't look
as good and you're bound to crush some of your tender crop, so I
like to use wooden flats. Wash them after each use.

Bugs a Problem?

If you suspect any bugs in your lettuce heads, wash them thoroughly. Nothing will kill a sale quicker than the owner (or, heaven forbid, a diner) finding a worm or slug in your produce. The commercial growers are way ahead of you in this respect because they use so much insecticide. They have to, in order to produce a bug-free harvest. You have to produce the same clean harvest, but since most of you will be growing organically or using limited insecticides due to their cost, you must spend extra time searching for bugs.

Some books suggest dunking the produce in a strong salt water solution; this supposedly loosens the bugs' grip and makes them fall off. Rinse carefully in clean water.

If your produce is infested with bugs, don't deliver it. Either use it yourself or send it to the mulch pile, but don't take a chance on sending it to a restaurant. The only other alternative, and it's a time-consuming one, is to take the heads apart and inspect each leaf as you wash it. Since this is what the restaurant is going to do, maybe you can strike up a deal whereby you furnish the salad ingredients to them cleaned and sorted. They might even allow you to do it in their preparation room with sinks and lots of running water.

Vine Crops

Time to learn how to pick tomatoes, cucumbers, and squash. It's a good idea to cut the stem rather than trying to pull or twist the fruit off. Keep your clippers handy. In fact, one good idea is to sew a holder onto all your jeans or overalls. It's like having a holster for your six-shooter. You can whip out those clippers whenever you need them. You can even add a decorative touch by doing a little embroidery or needlepoint on the patch, such as your initials or a carrot in bright colors.

A patch sewn on your trousers makes a handy pocket for your clippers.

Back to your vine crops. Pick only the red ripe tomatoes and the medium-sized cucumbers and squash; wash them and lay them carefully in the flats. You must be very careful in handling these vegetables so they aren't bruised. Don't fill a flat halfway and then pick it up so they all roll about, bumping into each other. You're not harvesting pool balls, you know. One easy solution is to place crumpled newspaper in the bottom of each flat. These crops shouldn't be stacked more than two deep. Arrange them so they look good, with your best on top. You can sort them into small, medium, and large boxes, but if they look too uniform, the restaurant may confuse them with a commercial shipment.

There's no bending over when you harvest most vertical crops.

A lot of you will question handling the produce so carefully. If the commercial grower can pick by machine, send tomatoes rolling down a ramp, and drop them into a pile two feet below, then sort them by dropping them another two feet through various size holes, why can't you? I think you know the answer. Their tomatoes are bred to withstand tough treatment; they're also picked while still green and hard. Why do you think supermarket tomatoes taste the way they do? You're producing something special, so treat it as such.

Cucumbers and squash have to be picked at least twice a week or they'll get too big while you're not looking. In fact, you'll always come across one or two that you missed during the last picking and now are too big. Don't be tempted to include them in your harvest. I know they weigh a lot more and would be very profitable, but you've promised to deliver choice produce—something no one else can do—so stick to that promise. Throw the excess in the compost pile or use it on your table. You wouldn't give an oversized, bitter, pithy cucumber to your best friend, would you? Well, do the same in your business. Only the best for your restaurant. Let them know it, too. They're paying for it and they deserve to be reminded in a nice way that they're getting only the very best.

Bush Crops

You can classify peas and string beans, or snap beans as they're called nowadays, as either vine or bush crops depending on the variety, but you pick them the same way. With your basket ready (a wooden mushroom basket is a good size), and clippers drawn, snip off all beans of medium size and drop them into the basket or a harvest apron if you have one. There are many harvesting devices on the market these days, from pails and baskets that you can strap on to bags that fit on your hand like a glove. They're all useful and you might decide to invest in one or more if your volume warrants the expense.

The same caution applies to oversized beans as well as cucumbers: don't include them in your harvest. Why spoil a nice basket of string beans with a few large, bulging pods? Eggplant and peppers are next. Use your clippers and handle the fruit carefully. Get everything out of the sun as soon as possible.

By the way, that applies to you also. On a hot, sunny day, wear a hat to keep your head shaded. You're just like those vegetables (I don't mean an eggplant) that wilt in the sun after an hour or so. You both need a little water and lots of shade while you're waiting to go to the restaurant.

Cabbage Family

This is harvested in the same way as the leaf family: for broccoli, cauliflower, or cabbage, cut one head at a time, taking lots of leaves with each head (they look great that way). Check for worms, wash in salt water if necessary, and pack in flats.

Keeping Count

The easiest way to keep count is to add to your total as you place the rinsed and cleaned items into the flats. Keep a grease pencil and plastic score card tied together so you can jot down the numbers after finishing each bed or vegetable. Paper and pencil won't work very well; it's wet when you harvest, and water will make a mess of any system except the grease pencil and plastic. Writing numbers on the flats is confusing when you reuse them. A very simple system is to buy an 8½" x 11" plastic folder in any dime or stationery store. On a sheet of white paper, list your plant varieties with room next to each for adding the numbers in the field. (Leave lots of room for the numbers because you tend to write big when your hands are wet and cold.) If you insert a piece of cardboard, your chart will be stiff enough to write on without bending. Each day's tallies can be wiped off with alcohol or cleaning fluid. One further suggestion: punch a hole in one corner and tie the grease pencil on the chart with a two-foot length of string. You could also buy a clipboard to hold the plastic chart and tie the pencil to the clipboard.

Weighing

It's time to assemble your harvest and make up your delivery slip. Everything should be counted and packed neatly and artistically in the flats. Weighing should be done at this time. There's no need to take vegetables out of their flats. Weigh the whole thing and subtract the weight of the flat, which you've figured out beforehand. After you weigh the empty boxes, note the empty weight on the side of each one with a waterproof Magic Marker, and you'll be set for the entire summer.

Enter the weights of your produce on your plastic score card, then add everything up before filling out your delivery ticket. You may want to adjust the numbers or weights slightly. No, I don't mean upward. You can adjust them downward, to take into account any undersized or less-than-top-quality produce. The other way to handle these items is to adjust the price downward to reflect the quality. It all depends on how many you're including and how inferior or small they are. One easy way to count undersized items is to give two—or even three, if they're really small—for the price of one. Here's another method: let's say you had to pick all the lettuce in a particular bed because it was going to bolt soon or you didn't want to keep the bed open for just fifty scattered heads. You could include them in the delivery, counting each head as you rinse and pack them. Then adjust your final tally by deducting 10 percent of the final tally. Or you might drop the price by five or ten cents per head. Just be careful that you don't continually give away your profits.

Pricing and Delivery Ticket

Once you have a total count by weight and number of heads, consult your current price lists. (Review chapter six if you've forgotten how to keep abreast of current prices.) These should be updated weekly, particularly if the seasons are changing and out-of-season items are coming or going. In order to save time, your delivery ticket should be made out ahead of time (the night before a delivery day, for example) with the items and unit prices, so all you have to do is fill in the pounds and number of heads and multiply by the unit price. This is easily done with an inexpensive pocket calculator. Don't try to do it longhand; there are too many calculations to do while your vegetables sit there begging to "go to market" before they wilt and get rubbery. Your ticket should be short and sweet. Keep it to one sheet of paper and be sure it's legible. As I suggested, a bank deposit slip is just the right size for about fifteen items. Always make a carbon copy for your files.

If you have a partner who helps with the harvesting, you can fill out the delivery ticket while he or she is loading the produce. If your vehicle is parked in a cool, shady spot, I suggest you fill out the delivery slip after you load and clean up. You'll probably want to wash up and throw on a clean shirt and shoes, and it's a good time to sit down and rest for a minute. If your produce is better left unloaded until just before leaving, do the calculations first, but try to keep the ticket clean and dry. It tends to get pretty soggy and messy in the garden.

Packing and Loading

Time to get your delivery ready to go. Once everything is packed, arrange it in your van or car in a way that will prevent crushing, sliding, or falling. Spread everything out, stacking only what you have to, and pack the flats in tightly so they won't slide off one another. Keep the top layer of each flat as attractive as possible. If you have a pickup truck, cover your produce with a heavy canvas so the wind won't whip and tear the lettuce. Make sure items such as tomatoes or eggplant can't roll around in their flats. If the flat isn't full, add something else so everything fits snugly. You're only going a few miles, but a tomato rolling around in a wooden flat can look pretty bad after ten or more corners and stops.

Before you leave, check your time so you know how long the harvest took. Mark those hours on your copy of the delivery ticket. It will help you plan your time and will give you a better idea of which vegetables take longer to harvest. When you return from making the delivery, you might also want to note how long that took. Someday, when your cash gardening business has made you rich, you may want to hire someone to do your harvesting and delivery for you. Then you'll have an accurate idea of how much time this part of the business requires.

Chapter 16

Year-round Production (well, almost)

$\boxed{\$}$ If you want to extend your growing season, move south. A slightly easier alternative is to create a "southern" environment where you live. You can do this by extending your own spring and fall seasons by approximately two to four weeks.

I'll admit that doesn't sound like much, but let's consider these statistics: the average gardening season is about six months—the last half of April, all of May, June, July, August, and September, and the first half of October, which is twenty-six weeks. If you start two weeks earlier, say at the beginning of April, and finish two weeks later, at the end of October, those four weeks have increased your growing season by 15 percent. If this still doesn't sound like much, just picture your present salary being increased by 15 percent.

Now, if you could extend the growing season by *four* weeks at each end, that would be a 30 percent increase, which is something really worth considering. Unfortunately, that wouldn't automatically increase your cash sales by 30 percent, because the beginning and end of the growing season are not as productive as the middle. So we might realistically expect a 20 percent increase in sales from a 30 percent increase in season length, which is still a worthwhile goal.

Of course, in the more southern states, the growing season is much longer than twenty-six weeks, so the percentage advantage of extending the growing season is not as much. However, just the opposite is true the farther north you go. As the frost-free growing season becomes shorter, those extended two to four weeks at the beginning and end of the growing season could become extremely valuable.

Here's another point to consider: in later winter and early spring, you're just dying to get outdoors and get started. It's a very enjoyable and exciting time of the year for a gardener. And in the fall, the weather is so perfect that even though you're winding down from a hard summer of gardening, it's still a time to relax and enjoy the outdoors. If you capitalize on your own enthusiasm, you'll wind up increasing your productivity.

Protection Needed

Both spring and fall weather can be quite erratic, however. So you need protection from the elements, which is fairly easy and inexpensive to provide, and a little ingenuity, which is free.

Let's consider each season. In the early spring, it's important to get that soil warmed up. It's been freezing all winter, so we have to protect the garden soil from chilly nights and sudden drops in temperature, while allowing the sunshine to come through. We also want to protect it from any chilly rains and late-season snows or frosts. All that's needed is a clear plastic cover stretched over our familiar wire frame (chapter three). The frames don't have to be very tall, because nothing is growing under them yet. Tilt the frames a little so the water will drain off outside your beds. Usually at this time of the year, we do not want to add any more water to the soil. We want it to start drying out as well as warming up. (If you have a compost pile, do the same thing: cover it with clear plastic and let it start warming up.) If you've laid down mulch or other covering to protect your soil through the winter, remove it before you put on the clear plastic.

Test Soil Moisture

If you didn't prepare any of your garden beds last fall, don't be afraid to do it in early spring, providing the soil is not too wet. The standard test for soil readiness is to squeeze a handful. If it drips, it's too wet; if it won't form a ball, it's too dry. But if it forms a ball in your fist and then breaks apart easily when you poke it, it's ready to be worked.

Now is the time to add lots of compost (remember to check your pH beforehand) and turn your soil. If you're planting seeds, make sure the surface soil is fairly fine and uniform. Rake it smooth and level, then cover it with your wire and plastic protection. If you expect heavy winds, tie the wire frames down so they won't blow away. The best idea is to nail or staple the wire to your wood frames, and attach the plastic to the wire either with clothespins or by stabbing the wire through the plastic before you attach the wire to the frames. The ideal structure is a slight arch. It leaves an air space between the soil and the plastic wire cover and will allow the heat to build up inside and be retained at night.

Weeds Are a Good Sign

Once you see weeds growing, you know your soil is warming up fast. Reach in under the frames with an action hoe and cut off those weeds periodically so they don't take all the nutrients from your soil. There's no need to remove them after you cut them off. Just leave them on top of the beds to become part of your mulch.

When you start planting your seeds, you can continue to use these same structures. Lift up one side of the wire and plant your seeds at their proper spacing. Sprinkle with a watering can, making sure to use sun-warmed water, and replace the cover. Now you have to be careful, because the sun gets extremely warm in spring, and heat can build up rapidly in an unvented structure. If the soil gets too warm, the seeds will cook and never germinate. A simple method of venting your covers is to cut slits in the plastic or fasten one end open with clothespins.

But as you vent your covers, the moisture could evaporate too quickly and your seedlings could dry out from the heat. One solution is to cover or replace the clear plastic with black plastic, whichever is easier. This will prevent the heat from building up. Contrary to popular belief, black plastic will not increase the temperature underneath as much as clear plastic will. Although many gardening experts recommend laying down black plastic "for heat-loving plants," the real reason for using black plastic is that weeds will not grow underneath it because of the lack of light. The sun's rays cannot penetrate black plastic. With clear plastic or glass, on the other hand, the rays strike the ground and reflect back, but not through the plastic or glass, causing the "greenhouse effect." So using black plastic to cover the frames will work effectively for newly planted seeds. If it's fairly tight, it will keep the moisture inside, preventing the top layer of soil from drying out.

But you must be extremely cautious; check your beds twice a day. As soon as the seedlings sprout, they must get sunlight or they will become leggy. One simple reminder is to plant a few of the same seeds three or four days before you plant the rest. When those sprout, you know you have to remove the top because the others will be sprouting in just a few days. Those seeds are sacrificed in order to save the rest of the crop from becoming too leggy to be productive.

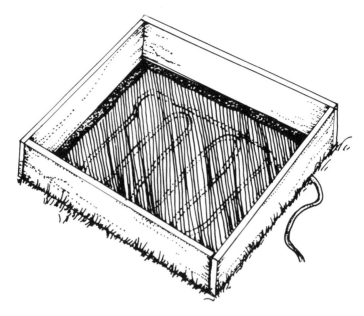

A heating pad or a heating cable can be used to get an early
start in the spring.

Heating Cables

If you *really* want to start early, and I mean more than a month
earlier, lay down heating cables or heating mats in your beds. Set
them about four inches under the soil surface. Of course, you have
to consider the cost of electricity versus the advantages of getting off
to an earlier start. And although this will enable the seeds to sprout
much more quickly, after they come up you'll have to keep the area
above them warm enough so that late winter cold spells don't do
them in. A lot depends on how adventurous you are. You might
want to try this as an experiment with a few crops to see how it
works out the first year.

In all your activities, keep in mind that you're trying to warm
things up early. Obviously, you won't use cold water or open your
covers on cold, windy days. And you might even want to make some
emergency covers for your frames out of old blankets which you can
throw on in case of a cold snap at night. Most of these ideas are just
common sense applied to a gardening situation. You want to
increase the temperature a little earlier than nature planned.

Procedures in Fall

In the fall, the situation is just the opposite. You're not concerned about below-ground temperatures because your soil is still very warm from the summer and takes a long time to cool off. You want to control the above-ground or air temperature. Since the plants are quite large and you're trying to keep them growing, you have a large volume of air to control, which requires a higher structure or cover.

In the fall, harvest can be continued if crops are protected from those first killing frosts.

And since the sun can be extremely warm on fall days, you've got to provide venting to prevent temperature buildup, which will cook your plants or bring your harvest too quickly. Many of the cool weather vegetables such as the lettuce and cabbage family will bolt to seed if the temperature in their enclosures is too warm. Most of the cool weather vegetables are hardy, so unless you're protecting something like lettuce from an evening freeze, you might not want to put up a cover.

Here's a chart of those vegetables that can withstand some frost:

FROST-HARDY CROPS

Beets	Cauliflower	Radishes
Brussels sprouts	Carrots	Spinach
Broccoli	Kale	Swiss chard
Cabbage	Lettuce	Turnips

Install Frames Early

Ideally, you should have the wire frame installed ahead of time so that you can cover your beds at a moment's notice if the weatherman predicts a frost, and uncover them just as quickly the next morning. Depending on the crop, you may want to cover them with blankets or plastic as you did in the spring, instead of frames, or you may want to provide a heavy mulch cover, allowing the top leaves of the plants to peek through. It will protect the fruit from freezing, yet will expose the plant tops to the sun every day. If you use a mulch cover of hay or leaves it should be light and airy so that moisture is not trapped, which can cause the plant to deteriorate or turn moldy.

For some crops, you might want to consider installing a heating mat under the soil. For example, radishes: the tops are quite hardy and with additional bottom heat and a heavy mulch once the plants are half-grown, you could extend their growing period into the cold weather. Again, weigh the cost of electricity against your anticipated profits. If you are considering a fall harvest, and you want to extend the season by two to eight weeks, you have to plan carefully when to plant and when to start providing protection. Of course, no one knows exactly when to expect the first frost or freeze, but by using your frost charts, you can do some fairly intelligent guesswork.

Put your wire frame in position in the fall. That way, when a frost threatens, you can quickly cover the frame with plastic.

These Keep Growing

Many crops will continue growing into the cold weather months, although slowly, if they're provided with the barest minimum of protection. These include spinach, Swiss chard, and many varieties of leaf lettuce. The root crops are most adaptable to a winter harvest, as long as you protect the ground from freezing while enabling the tops to continue growing slowly. Usually the only thing required is a mulch of hay or leaves, which allows the tops to peek out. Some crops, including kale and Brussels sprouts, actually improve in cold weather: the autumn freezes sweeten the taste. In fact, it is sometimes recommended that these not be harvested until after the first heavy frost. Here again, your wire frame covers will come in handy.

If you're going to extend your harvest all the way into the winter, you can leave it in its original location, protected by a heavy mulch, or move it to a more protected area. Carrots and potatoes can be dug and stored in moist sand in a cool spot such as your garage or they can be refrigerated. Use this technique to store a very large crop of something such as carrots and you can supply your customer all through the winter. The object here is to supply a crop so far out of season that it will command an extremely high price. This is what makes all your extra efforts worthwhile. On the other hand, you may have lost one of your biggest selling points, namely freshly harvested produce. Are you now merely competing with the food industry, which harvests huge quantities and stores them so they can be delivered year-round? If so, you're not going to win. Your stored carrots can't compete with out-of-season carrots from another part of the country. The only way you have a fighting chance is if your buyer insists on organically grown or local produce.

Growing Under Glass

Then there's growing "under glass." There's nothing wrong with this, but make sure you can produce enough to keep your buyer interested. It's a lot of work to set up a greenhouse environment, even if it's just cloches or a series of plastic-covered wire frames. Finally, remember your original objective of supplying 10 to 20 percent of your buyer's needs. If you drop down to just a few percent, you're going to hurt your future summer business as the buyer may feel it's not worthwhile to fool with such a small amount.

Some crops are more profitably sold out-of-season than others, but you may be put to a lot of extra work and expense to produce those out-of-season harvests. Other things are always so readily available year-round because they're grown in different parts of the country so it's tough to compete.

The last point to consider is that it's probably time you had a rest. As the popular song says, "You got to know when to hold them and know when to fold them." So quit while you're ahead!

Even if you live in Florida or along the coast in southern California where you could easily grow all winter long, maybe you need a little rest from your business.

Chapter 17

Expanding Fast: Go Big But Don't Dig

$\boxed{\$}$ So you have some big ideas about expansion. Well, why not, if that's the direction you're inclined to go. If you've been successful in your backyard growing and selling for the past year, it seems natural to expand. That's why companies grow. Success promotes growth, or at least the desire for growth.

Two important notes of caution. First, be sure you have had a successful full year under your belt before you think of expanding. It's important to know all the ins and outs of a business before you try to expand it.

Second, if you were content this past year with growing in your yard and delivering to your local restaurant, stop right there. Don't go any further...don't even read any further. Enjoy your free time and your extra income, and forget about expanding. Expansion brings problems. Why go out searching for problems? Enough will find your address without your driving up and down the street looking for more.

Of course, besides being harder to handle, a larger organization usually brings in more money, so if that's what you need to satisfy your needs (or your ego)—who am I to stop you? I'll even help you down the road in this chapter with some additional ideas and suggestions. Here are some factors to consider before making your decision.

1. **What kind of person are you?** Were you born to be in a crowd, or are you perfectly happy alone? Do you like to travel, or are you content to putter around the house (or garden)? Are you eager to sell someone on a new idea or shy about approaching others?

During this past year, were you happier in your garden growing or at the restaurant delivering?

2. **What kind of work do you like best?** Are you happiest when planning the garden layout and ordering seeds, digging, planting and harvesting, delivering produce, keeping charts and records, or counting money, banking, and filling out government reports and forms? (Or was the high point of the past year simply reading this book?)

3. **How successful were you, and what seems to be the potential in your area?** Are there lots of restaurants, lots of people, lots of gardeners, or just lots of nothing for miles around?

Your decision on whether to expand depends a lot on your answers. You probably can tell from your answers to the questions in 1 and 2 whether you're suited to expansion. But even if your answers indicate that you're unsuited to having a larger business, you can still expand—as long as your answers to the questions in section 3 were positive—that is, if you were successful and there is potential for growth in your vicinity. If you're happy and good at gardening, get someone else to handle the business or expansion end, to sign up new restaurants, and do the delivery. (Conversely, you might get someone else to grow vegetables in your yard or theirs, and you handle the business end.)

Ways to Expand

Keeping these things in mind, here's a whole bunch of ways to expand:

1. **Get others to work for you** at either end of the business so you have more time to do the part you prefer. Carried to the extreme, you'd simply be a manager, hiring a local gardener to do the growing in your yard and someone else to do the selling and delivery. Of course, there won't be much profit left for you, but you don't have to do much work. You control the idea and it's your business. You could also consider hiring a second or third person to garden for you from *his* yard, and hire any help needed for delivery. Now your operation becomes larger. This idea at any scale is particularly good for those who have experienced a change in their circumstances: a woman who becomes pregnant,

for example; a man who becomes disabled; or anyone who starts a new job with different hours. All of these people can still carry on the square foot gardening program. They become *managers* and run the operation at any size they desire.

Whom to Hire

When you get others to work for you, pick honest, reliable, capable people who are neither friends nor relatives. Hiring the right person is quite a process, and it pays to spend some time at it. (It's actually more time-consuming than complicated.) It involves advertising, screening the applicants, looking at their gardens and/or delivery vehicles, narrowing the selection down to two or three people, trying them out, and then signing an agreement. This sequence can be done very casually over the fence, if you insist on considering neighbors. It's most important to see the person in action. I've found that there's sometimes a bit of a gap between what people tell you they can do and what they actually can do. No one lies, but often what we think of ourselves and our capabilities is not quite the same as what others perceive in us. So seeing is believing.

Start with a trial—you might even try two people at the same time with the understanding that one will be picked and the other will be on standby. An easy way to hold an informed trial is to ask your first candidate to come over and work with you for an afternoon or so "to see what it's all about." Offer to pay him or her by the hour, and mention that you're doing this with two or three persons you're considering. If you advertised in the paper and received eighteen replies, it doesn't hurt to mention this to the top candidates. They'll be pleased to know they're still being considered, and they might put out more effort to beat the competition. To protect your business, mention right at the start that, if hired, you expect them to sign an agreement not to compete in a similar business in the area.

Don't Explain Everything

Your ideas will be further protected if you keep the details of your business under your hat. Don't explain all the details of where you sell and what you charge. At first it will suffice to say, "I raise and sell vegetables and need some gardening help." If pressed for details, say, "That's a business secret," or better yet, "Those are all details of the business that I'll explain later."

You can learn a lot about a person in just a few hours of working next to him. Learning the same things may take days if you merely talk to him. For example, just about everyone will tell you that he's a fairly fast and efficient worker, but put five people to the same one-hour task and it will take them from thirty minutes to two hours. More important, some will do an inferior job and some a superior job, regardless of the time spent. The fastest aren't always the best.

When you have someone over, have specific things for him or her to do—a wide variety—and repeat those same things with each person you try so you'll have some comparison among them. Try such tasks as chart planning, soil preparation, seeding, watering, putting up fencing or cages, harvesting, and sorting. By the end of three hours, you'll have a pretty fair idea of this person's ability, speed, adeptness, and neatness.

And most important, you'll know whether you like this person and can get along with him. If you're a loner and this person is a talker, he'll drive you crazy within a few weeks. Even if you don't plan to work side by side every day, congeniality is still very important. It's also important that he likes you and the work he'll be doing.

Before he leaves, you might ask him how he likes this work and if he's still interested in doing it. His enthusiasm (or lack of enthusiasm) and the reasoning in his answer will tell you a lot.

Making a Decision

After the trial run, say that you have other persons to see before deciding, but you'll let this person know within a certain number of days. And make sure you do let him know. That's only fair. Do this with at least two people, as things can come up and you often need that second person right away: your first person suddenly moves, gets sick, decides he doesn't like the work, isn't as good as you thought, has to fly to L.A. to visit a sick mother...who knows? Have a second person in the wings, all tested, experienced, ready, and willing to take over. This saves a lot of searching and talking all over again in case of an emergency.

A simple agreement merely states what each party agrees to do (and not do) and protects you a little from future problems. Notice I say "a little," because if someone wants to move suddenly or walk off the job, your agreement that states "forty-five days' notice" doesn't mean a thing. They're gone and you're left holding the bag—in this case, your piece of paper. What it does do is make sure you both start out understanding and agreeing to the same conditions. You should also put in a paragraph that he or she won't compete in any manner within a radius of _____ miles for _____ years. Although agreements aren't foolproof, I've found that once someone signs his name to something, he will usually adhere to those conditions. Of course, a dishonest or unscrupulous person will do whatever he pleases, with or without an agreement. Here's a suggested agreement:

EMPLOYEE'S AGREEMENT

I agree to work diligently at raising vegetables for _____ spending approximately _____

_{owner}
hours a week. My schedule will be flexible but I agree to be present on established harvest days.

In addition, I will spend whatever time is necessary to keep the garden in good productive shape, knowing this schedule will change through the growing season.

I agree to act as a subcontractor—self-insured, self-taxed, and self-sufficient. I will hold free from any liability the landowner, other participants including _____

_{owner}
and any others connected with this business.

Payment for my labor will be $_____ per hour worked ($_____ per week). Payment will be made by check weekly on Saturday noon.

Although I will supply my own tools and personal items, all seeds, plants, equipment, and related items including harvests belong to _____ .

_{owner}
All ideas, records, and data remain the property of _____ and I agree not to compete in a

_{owner}
similar business within a radius of ten miles for at least three years, whether I'm still working here or not.

Either party may terminate this agreement within thirty days by giving written notice.

_____
name

_____
Social Security number

_____
date

Payments

There are several ways to pay these new workers. You could make them partners and give them a share of the profits—with the percent of the take depending on their involvement. There are three possible variations on this method. You can deduct all your expenses and then give them a share of what's left (the net profits), you can give them a percent of whatever money is taken in (gross profits), or you can get very complicated and award them their percentage on a sliding scale (the more they raise or sell, the higher percentage they get).

Or you could simply pay them by the hour. Better yet, you could pay them by the week. Tell them you don't want to watch them or worry about how fast they work, when they come or leave, or how many rest breaks they take, you'll pay them $50 every week for six months to do whatever is necessary to grow this size garden. There are many advantages to this type of an arrangement for both parties—little paper work, few records to keep, but most important, it eliminates the clock-watching syndrome that many people get into. They begin to worry more about exactly what time it is than how well they are doing their job.

2. **Rent or buy additional land for a larger farm.** Now you can hire more people to work for you, and you'll have enough land to produce a big harvest. Remember, the square foot system doesn't require much land. You don't have to go out and buy ten acres. If one person can comfortably take care of 5,000 square feet working part-time, one acre (43,560 square feet) would require eight people. Allowing two extra for delivery and miscellaneous work, you could employ ten persons for every acre you farm. That's a lot of people.

If they all produced a good-sized crop from that land at our estimated rate of $5 per square foot of garden space, you could sell 43,560 X 60% efficiency X $5 per square foot = $130,000 worth of produce. If you paid them at 50 percent wholesale rates for their harvest, that would leave you $65,000.

Deduct the cost of your extra two people for harvesting and delivery (1,000 hours/season X $4/hour = $2,000 each) and you have more than $55,000 left for yourself, for six months' work. And that work involved no hard labor, no growing, no delivery—just organizing, supervising, and selling.

This is not to say that you won't have any headaches. You'll be employing ten persons, dealing with several major customers, and contending with the weather. Besides, could you find ten good people (and ten good customers)? I'll bet you could if you really wanted to and you hustled a bit. (Or how about just a half-acre, five people, and $25,000 profit?)

Finding Land

Back to the land. Where can you get an extra 5,000 square feet or up to an acre? Lots of places. Look around your town, or advertise in the newspaper. Stop in to see factories or businesses with extra land. Try a neighbor, or anyone with a large back or side yard. Look for empty lots. Since this is a business venture, you'll be willing to pay rent.

As you drive around your area, here are the basic things you'll be on the lookout for:

a. The ideal piece of land should be fenced, flat, and cleared. It should get sun all day and have a source of water nearby.

b. It should be accessible by car or truck, and should be geographically convenient to you and your helpers.

c. It should be reasonably secure from vandalism. Since you won't be living next door to keep a watch on it, be particular about its location and security. If it has one or more paths worn through it, don't use it. Neighborhood kids have a way of showing their resentment to anyone disrupting their normal short cuts. (If the path is made by deer or dogs, you're still in trouble.) Furthermore, a lush garden filled with a bumper crop of attractive vegetables is a great temptation to passers-by. Ask any vegetable or orchard farmer about his fields next to the road, and he'll tell you at length how fences, signs, and nasty words do nothing to keep the public out. They treat it like a public picnic ground.

d. It should have as reasonable a rent as possible. How much rent to pay? This varies so much throughout the United States and even within states that it would be foolish to give advice here. So much depends on whether you're in the city, the suburbs, or the country, as well as how much vacant land is available. One possible guideline is the rental asked of a small house for that neighborhood. The land should be about 10 to 20 percent of that value. For example, if you find a small two-bedroom bungalow on an average city lot (say 50' x 100') for $400 per month, you should be able to find an empty lot for $40 to $50 per month, or $500 to $600 per year. However, if someone owns an empty lot next to his home, he might be very happy to rent it for $200 to $300 per year, and you've got a bargain.

More expensive neighborhoods or those closer to cities might bring a much higher rental for that same two-bedroom bungalow. Now your land rental will be much more—but you've also increased your chances of finding more restaurants willing to pay higher prices. Remember, gross sales from each 5,000 square feet should be at least $25,000.

One other idea—do some horse trading. Offer the owner, especially if he lives next door, all the free vegetables he can eat in exchange for the use of the land. If you're dealing with a small family, you can't lose. Besides, they'll take an interest in the garden and keep trespassers out (and be less likely to trespass themselves).

When renting land, don't forget water. In most parts of the country water is still our cheapest utility, so you can be generous and offer to pay the owner's entire water bill for those six months. Just make sure they don't have a large swimming pool that gets filled every month.

e. It should have rich soil for this large-scale operation. Once you've narrowed your selection down to the two or three best bets, verify how good the soil is. You can do this by having the County Extension Service or local agricultural agent write up a report; you can buy some inexpensive soil test kits and dig samples from ten different areas, measure them, and see how they rate; you can ask three expert garden friends to look them over and get three completely different opinions; or you can do it the easy way—from your car. Look at what's growing there now. If you see a tangled, overgrown field of weeds three feet tall, that's your place. Weeds will grow in just about any soil, but you'll find they grow thickest where the soil is well-drained, rich with humus, and high in nutrients. You can get a pretty good idea of the natural growth of a lot in any season. If there are lots of young trees and bushes sprouting up, you know it hasn't been used in at least three years.

The next step is to dig five test holes, one in each corner and one in the middle. See how deep the top soil is, how many stones you find, and whether it's clay. How deep do the weed roots go? Next, see what's under the top soil. Is it hard pan (you almost need a pick to loosen it) or sandy material? Before you close up the holes, pour a bucket of water into each one and see how long it takes to drain. Drainage is very important for good vegetable growing.

Don't Worry About Weeds

Don't worry about how thick and deep the weeds are. When you have the lot plowed and rototilled, they'll be chopped up and mixed in with the soil—free humus the first year. Yes, their seeds will sprout and try to outgrow your garden, but we have ways of keeping them in check. I'd rather start with a rich soil with lots of weeds than try to grow in poor soil. It takes years and years to build up a poor soil but only one or two years to control heavy weeds.

When you dig those five holes, take five cups of soil (baby food jars are handy) for later testing. Those tests will tell you the present pH of the soil as well as how much NKP you'll have to add to raise a good crop.

This ideal piece of property may sound like a tough place to find, but don't be discouraged. There are lots of them in every town and village—even in cities. Set up a chart so you can rate and compare all the places you find.

3. **Start a chain.** Set up the idea in other communities, and manage it so you have someone to grow crops and someone to deliver. If the restaurant you deliver to is part of a small chain, ask if the other locations wouldn't like the same delivery. Then go to that location—usually at least twenty miles away—and set everything up with a local grower and delivery person for whom you have advertised in the local paper. If the restaurant isn't a chain, the owner will probably know the owners of many other restaurants in other communities. Ask him for suggestions and a recommendation and introduction to several others. Don't worry about becoming your own competition. This expansion into other communities won't affect your restaurant or your local business.

4. **Create a franchise.** This is the ultimate form of expansion. Advertise all over the county, state, or even country. You can sell franchises in any area with the use of your trademarked name. Include advice on how to get started: a starter package (consisting of a soil-testing kit, seeds, seed-starter soil and containers, a heating cable, a plastic enclosure, vertical growing frames, and watering devices); a how-to booklet, or, better yet, a copy of this book; a letter of introduction to restaurants in the area; a price schedule for their area; a membership sticker and wall plaque;

continuing advice in the form of a monthly newsletter and advice by mail; free plans for all wheeled equipment needed; etc., etc. Purchasers pay an initial fee and have exclusive rights to their neighborhood as well as the first two restaurants of their choice. Then they pay a small percentage of their sales to you, the parent company. They agree to inspections from the parent company, and agree to adhere to specified standards.

If it all sounds far-fetched, just remember that McDonald's started out this way with one restaurant in California. Just ten years ago, a McDonald's franchise cost $20,000. Today they charge over a half a million dollars just to use their name. Then you have to buy the land, build the building, and buy the equipment.

5. **Co-op.** Another method might be to expand your basic idea into a co-op in which you get several people to grow in their backyards. At the same time you sign up several restaurants. Then everyone brings his or her produce to a central point; it's counted for credit to the grower and then combined before delivery to the various restaurants. This way you'll have a fairly uniform amount. As one grower gets low on carrots one week, someone else probably has an excess. The more people you have, the more uniform your total harvest will be. You may be able to supply 50 percent or more of a large restaurant's needs along with several other smaller restaurants. The advantage to the restaurants is that they get a more uniform amount each week. They also have more protection from one person's disaster or wipeout. Your share of the proceeds is a small percentage of the total sales. You can still be one of the growers or just a manager now. Again, you need agreements and understandings. I hate to suggest it, but as you grow larger, you may need to hire a lawyer. Granted, they tend to complicate the operation, but they are there to keep you out of trouble. You're probably going to get more involved with the government at several levels, so you'll need some professional help.

6. **Think big.** Once you've expanded into a larger organization, why not diversify into other services and products as suggested in the next chapter. If you've incorporated into a company, why not have a division for each service? Just think, if you can sell vegetables to a restaurant, why not homemade cheese? Sooner or later, people you meet will offer their talents at cheesemaking, pickling, or sewing aprons. Many of the restaurants today have gift shops

or sell homemade items at the entrance. Why not yours? Pretty soon you'll have little old ladies working in all corners of the county, supplying your gift shop division with so much material you'll have to hire extra people to handle the collecting, delivery, and paperwork. Your bright lawyer will soon suggest a separate corporation and your accountant (oh, yes, I forgot to tell you, you're going to need an accountant by now) will nod in perfect agreement. Think of all the new work you'll be creating for them. One day your lawyer will show you how you can even do better if you set up a holding company for all those scattered independent corporations. Then you'll need a different holding corporation for your warehouse (didn't I tell you about that?) and it would make more sense for you to buy a little land (only ten acres or so) just in case you want to hire some migrant workers to farm right on your new property, rather than have all those homeowners digging up their backyards.

One night you'll wake up and shout, "Of course! A mail-order business!" You have your gift shop products, your diversified hobby division, your homemade cheeses—why not sell them all through a mail-order company? By now you'll be directing a mini-conglomerate replete with many diversified activities. Pretty soon you'll find that raising sunflower seeds takes too long—it's easier to buy them by the carload from some agribusiness out West. All you have to do is buy up a small bagging company in Minnesota and distribute them that way.

Most of you are probably smiling by now over this tongue-in-cheek story of your phenomenal growth, but I'll bet there are going to be at least one or two readers who will go on to similar achievements. More power to them, if that's what they want.

7. **Add new products.** Back to earth for most of you realists—how can you expand but not grow large? Easy. Try diversifying by offering or handling other products, but keep it on a small scale. Think of other products that are related to gardening which you can offer. The next chapter will discuss many of them, such as mushrooms, herbs, or special gourmet vegetables (artichokes, fennel, sea kale, leeks, endive, or watercress). How about utilizing your cooking abilities to make preserves, candied vegetables, dried fruit? I could go on and on, but what it all boils down to is this: if you want to expand, think creatively.

Many small roadside farm stands expand into offering a full line of fruits and vegetables by buying wholesale all fruits and vegetables that they don't normally grow or that are out of season. Thus, they can offer their customers full-stop shopping rather than what they can grow and harvest that week. I'm not suggesting you do that because you'd then be nothing but a small wholesale-retail grower and that's not the idea of square foot gardening.

But it does lead you to thinking of extending your growing season into the cold months. Why not extend your efforts into eight, ten, or even twelve months of harvests? No reason at all. Depending on your location, you should be able to get in at least a couple of extra months by following the chapter on digging a harvest all winter (chapter sixteen). In fact, all the ideas in the next chapter will enable you to expand your business into the colder months or to offer additional products from your land. Only you can decide if you want to expand, if it's worth all the effort involved. If it's worth it to *you,* then make your move. The point I've tried to make in this chapter is this: the opportunity *is* there, if you want it. If so, go for it.

Chapter 18

Expanding Slowly: Stay Small But Stand Tall

$ Once your business is under way, you will need to keep seeking out ways to improve it, both in terms of the efficiency of the operation and the net revenue. You're looking for the bottom line: you want to enjoy yourself, spending as little time as possible at the "drudgery" aspects of the work, yet realizing a fairly handsome return on your time and investment. Once the business is running smoothly, and that's usually after the first or certainly the second year, you should start to review your records and see how you can improve your business.

Which Crops Are Profitable?

Your first step should be to compare the time spent in planting, growing, and harvesting various crops, and to try to weed out (no pun intended) those that are unprofitable. Sometimes you have to keep certain "loss leaders" because they're popular, but see if you can't reduce the amount you deliver of that particular crop and increase the more profitable ones.

There are many factors to consider in identifying an unprofitable crop. How long does it take to plant? How pest-resistant is it? How difficult is it to grow? Does it require much time to water? How long does it take to grow to maturity? How long will it remain in the ground taking up garden space? How easy or difficult is it to harvest, and how well does it hold up after harvesting? Is the harvest time critical, or can it be left in the ground for another few days or even a week past maturity? Does the price fluctuate rapidly, or is it fairly stable throughout the growing season? Is it the type of crop that enhances your image—that is, can very few others supply it—or is it available almost anywhere?

How Secure Are You?

This brings us to the issue of job security. If you want your business to flourish, you have to provide something that no one else can. If your services or product can be secured elsewhere, you're going to have a hard time staying in business without cutting prices. Why? Because as soon as something can be obtained from two places, the decision of where to buy it usually boils down to price. Keep in mind that you're not necessarily equipped to compete on prices with anyone else; you're offering high-quality, fresh-picked produce.

Another aspect of building security is making sure that your customer is happy. Talk to him occasionally about the long-range potential. Remind him that you're not trying to supply him with everything, or even 50 percent of certain items, but that you're trying to help his business by supplying fresh, good-tasting vegetables that no one else can.

Can You Specialize?

Another important technique you can use to further your business is specialization. For example, some people have said, "Radishes are so easy and quick that I'm going to specialize in them. I'll become the radish king of my whole county." They then set out to grow two, three, even ten varieties. Others try just lettuce, and of course there are so many varieties that it's not hard to specialize in lettuce alone. Quite often this approach will work out fairly well, because a person can furnish varieties that no one else is able to, and can become quite expert at growing one particular crop. Aside from the potential disaster of a disease or pest wiping out his entire crop, he might profitably enjoy this idea of specializing. And, whether you confine yourself to one crop or grow a few, specialization certainly makes all your planning and growing a lot easier. It's probably best to consider this after you've been in business for a year or two.

Any Leftovers?

Another idea for increasing your income is to try selling your leftover harvest. Of course, we started out with the idea that your customers are going to get only the very best, the choicest of your harvest. But what about the runners-up—the undersized or mis-shaped, the ones slightly damaged by pests? Of course, the first idea is to use those in your own household. They are free groceries.

If you have enough of them, you might consider some other ways of disposing of them. You might tell your prime buyers that you will throw them in for nothing as a gift, but that idea usually backfires. Soon they expect that, or they may feel that your regular prices are too high. You might sell them at half price, but then that may again affect the price of your main crop. It would probably be best to sell them to a different source. Here's where a neighborhood outlet is quite functional. As long as the produce is not badly damaged or deformed, most people will take it at a reasonable price. You have the option of selling it for cash, or even of bartering it for someone else's goods or services.

How to Barter

Here's an idea I used when I started my business. I went to a local garage and said, "If you'll take care of my old pickup truck, I'll give you a basket of fresh vegetables every week." I continued to pay for my own gas and oil, but I got free tuneups, oil changes, new brakes, flat tires fixed, battery charges, just about everything except major repairs. All I had to do was pick out an assortment of fresh vegetables and deliver them in a large harvest basket every week. I made sure they were good-looking, but they didn't have to be the perfect ones that I was taking to my prime buyer.

I worked a similar barter with a local deli, so that twice a week my employees and I got free lunches, anything we wanted. Imagine going in to your favorite deli and, without any thought of cost, ordering anything you'd like. In exchange, we brought them a full harvest basket each time.

Of course, there will always be those crops that can't be sold. Some can't even be given to friends or neighbors. After all, you don't want to be thought of as producing poor-looking crops. But there is one place that will be very happy to accept everything you bring it, and that's your compost pile. Don't waste a thing that you grow.

Have Two Outlets

Another good way to expand slowly is to find two outlets for your product. This increases your job security and enables you to make better use of a fluctuating harvest. For example, suppose you have an unusually large harvest of any one thing. It may happen because of the weather, poor planning, or just overplanting. But if it's too much for one outlet it will go to waste. Here's when you can easily split it up if you have two customers.

Mushroom Crop

Have you ever thought of growing mushrooms in your cellar? They're relatively easy to grow, bring in a fairly good price, and require very little work.

Before deciding, you might buy one of the kits sold by mail order houses. They provide everything you need to get started on a very small scale. Give it a try before investing in a lot of equipment and soil. It takes some time to grow mushrooms, but once they start producing, they come along at a fairly uniform rate. Then it's just a matter of starting new batches on a regular schedule.

Fruits and Berries

If you'd like to earn lots of money in a very short time, but don't like being tied to daily or even weekly work and delivery schedules, consider growing fruits and berries. Many of them are fragile and do not ship well. This means that they're not always available to restaurants and stores, and when they are, they command a very high price. The season is short for local harvest, so it's tailor-made to your preferences.

You'll need a fair amount of room to grow these crops, but they do not require much tending or care throughout the year. If you have a lot of room and want to increase your income, you might add fruits and berries to your square foot garden. This would involve a lot more work during the harvest period, but you'll probably be able to fit it in with your normal schedule.

Strawberries

Strawberries can be grown in your square foot garden beds, planted four per square foot. We plant them that close because we're going to let the parent plants grow while snipping off all baby plants (runners). This allows the parent plant to set the maximum amount of fruit the following year.

You can choose the spring bearers, which produce just one crop per year, or the everbearing varieties, which produce a crop throughout the summer. Consult catalogs or your Extension Service for the best variety for your area. Prepare your soil with lots of organic matter, and be especially fussy when you're planting.

Depth of planting is critical: set too high, strawberry plants will dry out and die; set too low, they'll rot away. As far as pest control, be prepared to protect the plants from both above and beneath.

Moles and ground mice can tunnel underground and come up underneath, even if you have a bird cover over the top. If this happens in your area, you might consider lining the bottoms of your boxes with galvanized hardware cloth before you start adding the soil. If your soil depth is at least six inches, you'll have enough depth to plant in yet the roots can still grow deeply by penetrating the hardware cloth, but the critters can't come up from underneath and into your beds.

Wire frames covered with clear plastic create a greenhouse.

Another advantage to the wood-bordered bed method is that you can easily install frames or wire arches to cover your beds for protection from birds. You can then cover the wire frames with clear plastic in early spring, creating a greenhouse effect. This will get the plants off to a quick start and produce an earlier harvest. Later on you can cover them with bird netting. You might also want to cover them with vented plastic during inclement weather to keep heavy rains and possible mildew off your strawberries. Or, if you are experiencing a particularly hot, dry spring, you might want to use some shade film over your frames to keep your strawberry harvest from ripening too fast. Everything needs its own good time to ripen properly, and when it's too hot and dry, most of the fruit will remain small and poorly developed, and will be lacking in sweetness.

Keep in mind that strawberries are perennials and will occupy that space for the entire year, and the spring bearers will produce just one spring crop. However, that one crop will command a very high price. Each plant will yield well over a pint and at four plants per square foot, strawberries can produce a handsome profit of several dollars per square foot. Check your local prices and you'll get a better estimate.

Of course, the nicest part is that there's very little work the rest of the year. You'll be weeding, mulching, and fertilizing in the summer when the plants are setting their fruit buds for the following spring. Keep the runners trimmed and mulch after the first hard freeze to protect the plants over the winter. If you keep the runners or baby plants pruned off, your parent plants should produce for three to five years before they have to be replaced. The everbearing varieties will give you a smaller single harvest, but will produce over a longer period of time. In the southern regions of the country, only the spring-bearing varieties will grow properly.

Raspberries

Raspberries are another excellent cash crop which brings an extremely high yield during their two harvests per year (late spring and late fall). The fall crop is usually much larger and better. Raspberries require very little work other than keeping the vines upright, pruning yearly, and spraying occasionally to keep out diseases and pests.

You won't have any trouble selling this fruit, as it's in big demand everywhere in the country. The bushes take up a considerable amount of room, though, and should be planted in a four-foot bed, with the plants spaced two feet apart. They will send up many new shoots, resulting in a multitude of new stalks each year. These have to be thinned to no more than one per square foot. Since the fruit is so fragile, the shipping distance cannot be very long, and, as a result, you very seldom find these fruits in the market. When you do, they usually bring three to four dollars per half pint. When your bushes are producing, it doesn't take long to pick a half pint. Again, the annual cash yield per square foot will reach several dollars.

Blackberries

Another berry that produces a good yield is the blackberry. Although your yield will be larger than you'd get with raspberries, the price will be considerably less. That's because you're competing with many wild varieties in many parts of the country. Most people find it easier to pick wild blackberries than to grow their own. They should be planted at about the same spacing as the raspberries. They're not as fragile as raspberries, so you will find these in the market. But the demand is still there for fresh-picked blackberries, so if you have lots of room, go to it. Or, better yet, try to add cash to your income by locating a wild source. (Get permission if it's on someone's property.) Now you can let Mother Nature do all the growing for you (she's energetic) while you stick to harvesting and selling.

Blueberries

Blueberries are another good seller but require a considerable investment in both money and time. These berries grow on large bushes which take several years to develop. Because of their size, they're more difficult to protect from the birds. Then, just when you think you have everything covered properly, you'll find that mice, chipmunks, and squirrels will get in somehow and climb right up the stems and eat the fruit inside your bird netting, so you need protection from the ground up and right over the top.

Many people have ended up building a completely enclosed, screened cage to house their blueberry bushes. They can grow to be well over six feet tall, so we're talking about considerable time and expense. Blueberries must have a very acid soil and, like all berries, need a fair amount of sunlight. The bushes are heavily laden with fruit during early summer. You get one harvest per year. The plants require very little care once established, so if you have a large amount of property and can devote the space to these bushes, you may find yourself with a fairly good long-term investment.

Other Berries and Fruits

There are several other fruits or berries, such as gooseberries, currants, and boysenberries, which you might be tempted to consider. There's not as much demand for them, though, which means that the prices they'd bring would be correspondingly low. These are specialty crops, and would not be my first choice for your cash garden.

Dwarf fruit trees might be another consideration for those who have a large amount of property. The problem with these trees is that they take a considerable amount of care, particularly spraying, to bring the fruit to harvest without blemishes, worms, or disease spots. Pests, again, are quite a problem, from birds eating the cherries to chipmunks and squirrels climbing into the trees and pulling off the peaches, apples, or pears. With one harvest per year, none of the dwarf fruit trees would make a particularly good investment in terms of either money or time. They are certainly not recommended for small-space cash gardens.

Seedlings

Another cash crop is *seedlings*. As you're potting them up, it wouldn't seem like too much more work to have all your excess seedlings planted in six-packs and then have these ready for sale to other growers, either commercial or hobby. The problem is that once you start this, you're tempted to start planting extra seeds in order to have excess seedlings. This can take your time away from your cash garden and could seriously impair your ability to produce a good harvest for the primary business.

Have a good supply of seedlings ready to go at all times.

Another idea would be to pot up all your seedlings and grow them into *transplant* size for sale to neighbors or local nurseries. Here again, you're in a totally new business. There's lots of competition, but it may be worthwhile if you have the time.

Sprouts

Speaking of seedlings, you might even consider seed sprouting for sale to your restaurants. There's a big demand for sprouts. Although this is another entirely new business, it's something that's done indoors and can easily extend your income into the colder months, enabling you to continue your cash garden right through the winter. With sprouts, as with all my suggestions, a word of warning: be careful not to let your supplementary business interfere with your main business—the cash garden—especially during the peak growing season. Once restaurants, markets, or other customers become dependent upon you, they don't like to see the supply dwindle. If they're forced to go to a different source, they might not come back.

You can see there are many directions to go—move fast and grow big or take it easy and just improve your present business. In either case, you want to be in control of the situation and make sure it's not only efficient and profitable, but fun.

If you aren't going to enjoy your new business, why even start it? Having a small family-run or home business is the goal of so many people. Now that you have accomplished that step—make sure you sit back every so often and appreciate what you have.

Index